Tax Strategies for Ordinary People

Jeffery Palmer, ChFC

0278003-00002-00

Tax Strategies for Ordinary People

Published by:
90-Minute Books 302
Martinique Drive
Winter Haven, FL 33884
www.90minutebooks.com

Published in the United States of America

140902-001.2

ISBN-13: 978-0692523018
ISBN-10: 0692523014

For more information on 90-Minute Books including finding out how you can publish your own book, visit www.90minutebook.com or call (863) 318-0464

Here's What's Inside...

Introduction

> "How you save and invest today will
> determine your income tax bill in the future."
> ~Jeff Palmer

One of the things I find most concerning is when people retire completely unprepared. In a recent study it was concluded, 82% of pre-retirees have absolutely no retirement income plan. When you consider 8,000 baby boomers turning age 65 every day over the next 16 years, it's a huge concern that people are so unprepared. As Stephen Covey once said, "You must plan with the end in mind." This is very accurate statement regarding sustainable retirement income stream that must last a lifetime.

In preparing a retirement income plan, you must consider how assets are allocated due to the potential tax pitfalls that can occur when you begin harvesting income from your investments. Because the way you save and invest today will determine your income tax rate in the future. By allocating appropriately, you can enhance your retirement income by drastically reducing income taxes in the distribution phase of your retirement, in turn improving your lifestyle. Isn't retirement all about lifestyle?

I wanted to write this book to help people improve their retirement years. From my 25 plus years of experience, few people are prepared for retirement. Most individual's retirement nest egg is inadequate to sustain a 20 to 30 year retirement. I'm concerned that people are going to run out of money during their lifetime due to various factors such as the escalating cost of health care, a long-term care event, over spending, increased taxes, inflation, sequence of return risk, and poorly chosen investment allocations. This is most frightening when you consider that many people will run out of money during the most vulnerable stage of their life. I feel it is my life's calling to help educate people on how to create sustainable tax efficient retirement income streams that will last a lifetime. I hope this book will be enlightening and helpful as you pursue a secure retirement.

Source: Fidelity Retirement Redefined, 2012 *

Source: American Association of Retired Persons, 2011 **

Chapter 1

Be Prepared!

"For I know the plans I have for you," declares the
Lord, "plans to prosper you and not to harm you,
plans to give you hope and a future."

~Jeremiah 29:11

For many people, the dream of Financial Independence
is doing "what I want, when I want and how I want
within reason." The younger you are, the bigger the
dream! To most people, financial independence means
you are no longer bound by the clock of an employer.
You have the time, money and health to pursue
personal interests, travel, enjoy hobbies, spend time
with friends and family, volunteer in organizations
without worries.

Life in the future is going to be awesome! This
pleasurable dream of financial freedom becomes a
nightmare for many Americans due to their lack of
planning and financial discipline. The retirement
grenade as I call it explodes when individuals
underestimate the dangers that loom in retirement
planning. Contingency planning for the "what if's" is
necessary in War and it's equally as important in
preparing for retirement.

Every American has the freedom to pursue happiness
and a better life for themselves and their family. To
make this possible, it will take planning and paying
attention to the details in order to secure your

retirement. A disciplined savings plan during the accumulation years combined with strategic tax planning will help achieve a secure retirement. Unfortunately, many individuals under save for retirement. The consequence is that for the second half of their life, they will pay the price for their misgivings. Many simply don't understand the need to be financially savvy early in life in order to have a better life in the future. No one ever wants to be broke in their retirement years. Unfortunately, many will retire broke while others will barely be able to meet their needs. There is a lack of understanding that due to poor money habits and lack of direction will put them on the glide path for retirement destruction. A secure retirement is not a right; it comes with hard work. You can change your direction in life with guidance and discipline at any age. However, you must be willing.

I believe some of the greatest lessons in life come from observing people in what to do and what not to do. You can learn something from everyone.

This book has been written based off of those personal and professional experiences working as a financial planner with individuals on all economic fronts. Millionaires definitely do things differently than non-Millionaires. Those who have secure retirements definitely do things differently than those who do not.

Retirement Landscape

As I examine the retirement landscape, more and more people are becoming dependent on government benefits such as social security and Medicare with little in the way of savings to last them a lifetime. This dependency is at the back drop of potential cuts in the future as the Federal government attempts to deal with large deficits that may swell even bigger as the last of the Baby Boomers enter retirement. To fund this burden, one would surmise that the government may increase taxes in the future to deal with this problem. Being tax savvy with your investments may have an even greater importance in the future.

There is a misconception on how much money it takes to be financially independent during retirement. Building a retirement budget and pre- planning for contingencies such as long-term care events, higher taxes, inflation, sequence of return risk, etc. is essential in obtaining the answer to this complicated question. I find that people underestimate the amount of retirement assets needed to maintain a 20 to 30 year retirement.

When my grandfather retired at age 65, his life expectancy was only 76 years of age. Therefore, when he died at age 76, it didn't take a lot of funds to maintain an 11 year retirement. However, he didn't realize my grandmother would live to age 96. She went through their life savings and became dependent upon the charity of her kids to help provide for her care. People don't realize how much money they must accumulate to live for a long period of time without employment income. So squeezing every dollar from the tax "turnip" for retirement is very important.

Few people have ever heard of the information I am going to share with you in the following chapters, especially when it comes to dealing with tax issues in your retirement income years. By applying the principles in this book, you should be able to save substantial tax dollars helping reach your goals more effectively and efficiently for retirement.

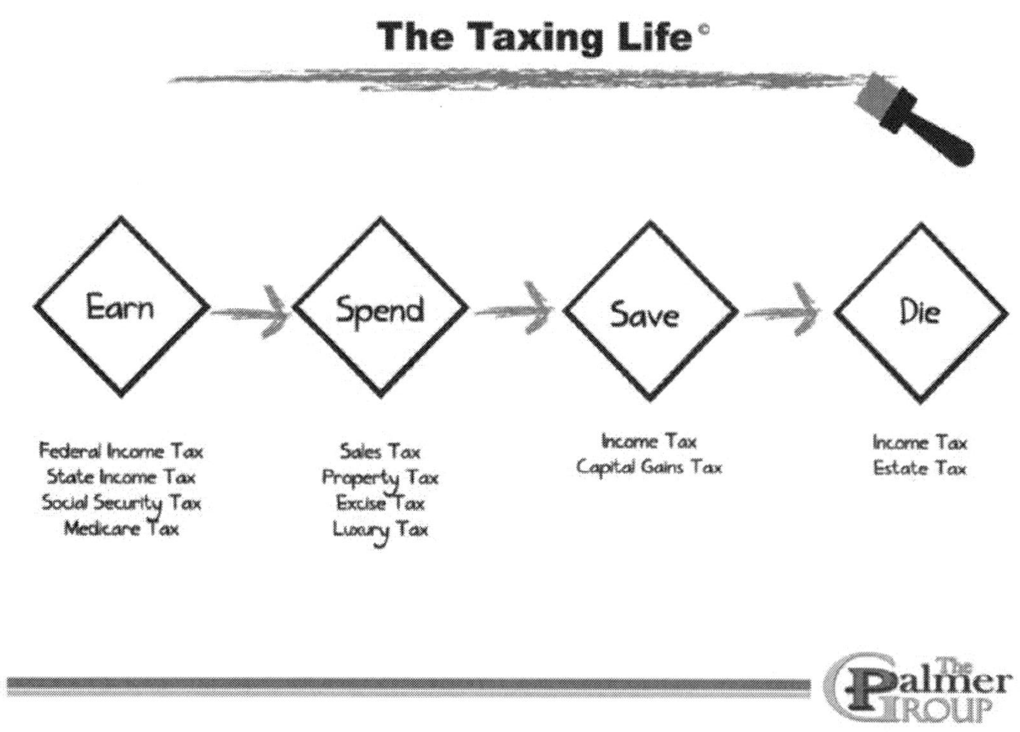
The Taxing Life ©
Earn
Spend
Save
Die
Federal Income Tax
State Income Tax
Social Security Tax
Medicare Tax
Sales Tax
Property Tax
Excise Tax
Luxury Tax
Income Tax
Capital Gains Tax
Income Tax
Estate Tax
The Palmer Group

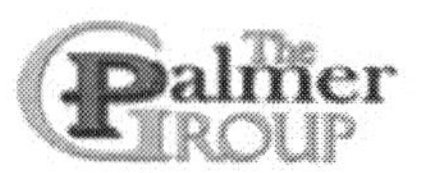

Chapter 2

The Taxing Life

"Certainty? In this world nothing is certain but death and taxes."

~Benjamin Franklin

At the beginning of the retirement savings journey, you must decide on the tax structure to invest in that will give you the greatest reward in the retirement income years. In order to understand which strategy or strategies to employ, a review of the income tax system is important. We will begin with the basics and move into more complex ideas as we progress. Please don't try to implement these ideas on your own. I'm providing you with enough information to explain the concept, but there could be tax rules that are not discussed within the following pages. Consult your CPA or Financial Planner to ensure these ideas will work in your particular situation

The Government has four ways to tax you. They tax you as you earn your money, spend your money, save your money and when you die with your money. As you earn your money, there is a federal and state income tax system. The federal income tax system is a progressive tax, beginning at 10% and increasing to 39.6% for the wealthiest tax payers. There is a misconception regarding the progressive income tax system. Higher income taxpayers are also subject to a 3.8% tax on their investment income.

Many individuals believe if they are in a 28% income tax bracket all of their income is taxed at 28%. This is incorrect due to a portion of your income being taxed at different percentages based on income bracketing. For example, a portion of your income will be taxed at 10% up to the first threshold and 15% to the next threshold before reaching the 28% tax bracket. Some states, such as North Carolina, impose an income tax, but other states such as Florida and Tennessee have no state income tax.

As you earn your money, you have a social security tax which is 6.2% and if you are self-employed, you can multiply the tax by two up to an annually adjustable threshold. The Medicare tax is at 1.45% on an unlimited amount of income and if you are self-employed, the employer, which is you, must match the 1.45%. For higher incomes, you can add an additional .9% for Obamacare. As you can see, the government is confiscating a pretty decent amount of your hard earned income up front.

As you spend your money, there's a sales tax on goods and services that you purchase. There are property taxes on your home and automobiles. There's an excise tax on gasoline, cigarettes and alcohol. We call this the "sin tax". In addition, there is a "luxury tax" on purchased selective luxury items. As you save your money, the income and growth of the assets may be taxed. Investment income from assets such as certificates of deposit (CD), money market accounts, taxable bonds, etc. are taxed at ordinary income tax rates. For example, if you earn 5% in a CD with an income taxpayer in the 30% federal and state income tax bracket, 1.5% of your rate of return will be confiscated by the government.

The capital gains taxation is broken down into short-term and long-term capital gains.

The short-term capital gains tax is taxed at your ordinary income tax rate due to the holding period being less than twelve months. Let's assume you purchased a publicly traded stock for $50 per share and it appreciated to $60 per share when you sold, the $10 profit will be taxed at your income tax rate versus the lower long-term capital gains rate. To be considered for long-term capital gains treatment, your holding period must be twelve months or longer. Furthermore, it's a tiered system in which the 10% and 15% tax brackets pay absolutely no capital gains taxes. The 25%, 28%, and 33% tax brackets pay a 15% capital gains rate and the 39.6% pay a 20% capital gains tax rate. In addition, if your income is above an income threshold, an additional 3.8% tax is assessed due to Obama Care. Lastly, most dividends are taxed at the same tax rates as long-term capital gains.

As you die with your money, certain assets can be taxed at ordinary income tax rates such as IRA's and non-qualified annuities transferred to beneficiaries. In addition, if you are one of the fortunate few that have sizable estates, your family could owe estate taxes when both spouses die.

The threshold to pay estate taxes is quite high today requiring few individuals to pay this onerous tax. If you do, the tax is 40% on the amount in excess of the estate tax exemption.

How Life Is So Taxing!

Let's illustrate an example of how a taxpayer will fare living to life expectancy under the four stages of taxation: Earn, Spend, Save and Die. I hope this illustration will provide a shocking truth about the burden the higher income taxpayers undertake.

Also, this is an example with realistic estimates. The estimated taxes could be different depending on the state and city in which you live. Jack currently is a 30 year old self employed physician who earns $300,000 per year of income. He pays each year about $19,000 in Social Security tax and Medicare tax. He pays about $100,000 per year in federal and state income taxes. He has $180,000 per year left over for lifestyle expenses and savings. Let's assume he spends $100,000 per year on lifestyle expenses, thereby paying $4,000 per year in state and local sales tax. Jack owns two nice vehicles and pays $1,000 per year in property tax. Jack owns a nice home and pays $6,000 per year in property taxes. In all total, Jack is paying almost half of his income in various kinds of taxes.

Jack saves $25,000 per year in a taxable investment in his brokerage account. After money management expenses, his net return is 8% per year. Let's assume he invests in mutual funds with a 100% turnover ratio. One half of his investment returns are ordinary income and half of his returns are treated with long-term capital gains treatment. The government will take an estimated 1.92% of the investment return due to income and capital gains taxes. Let's assume the rate of inflation is 3%. His real rate of return on investment is 3.08% per year (return after taxes and inflation).

After 35 years of contributions, Jack would accumulate approximately $3,000,000 after taxes. Also, Jack saves

$40,000 per year in a safe harbor 401(k)/profit sharing program. He will accumulate an estimated $7,444,000 in which there are no taxes paid until he begins taking a retirement distribution at age 65. Jack lives in a nice home with a fair market value of $ 1,000,000 with an estimated 3% appreciation rate.

Jack retires at age 65 and begins taking a 5% distribution ($340,000 per year net after taxes) from his 401(k) and brokerage account. Let's also assume that Jack and his wife die at age 83. Their 401(k) account will have an approximate value of $11,244,000 and the brokerage account will have an approximate value of $3,800,000 at death.

Jack's home is valued at $2,813,000 assuming 3% appreciation. All total, Jack has done well for himself with an approximate net worth of $17,857,000.

Jack and his wife have an "I Love You Will" and both die in 2014 leaving their children an estimated **net estate of $11,000,000**, Jack's heirs paid an estimate of $2,870,000. in federal and state inheritance taxes and $1,800,000 in income taxes from his 401(k)/profit sharing plan. The estate taxes were due 9 months from the date of death.

At age 65, Jack's lifetime employment earnings

with a 3% inflation adjustment was estimated at

$18,200,000. He spent an estimated $11,000,000 for living costs and savings. The government would take an estimated $7,200,000 in income taxes. If Jack and his wife die at age 83, they have paid the government an estimated $2,870,000 in estate taxes with heirs paying an additional $1,800,000 in income taxes on his 401(k) plan.

In all total, Jack's lifetime tax bill is approximate $11,870,000. <u>This is truly a taxing life!</u>

Understanding the tax system, determining appropriate tax deductions and tax credits, strategically positioning assets for retirement and death, as well as being tax wise could mean millions of dollars of enhanced wealth for you and your family. You need to be tax vigilant with your hard earned dollars to build wealth and security for your family.

Three Buckets of Money ©

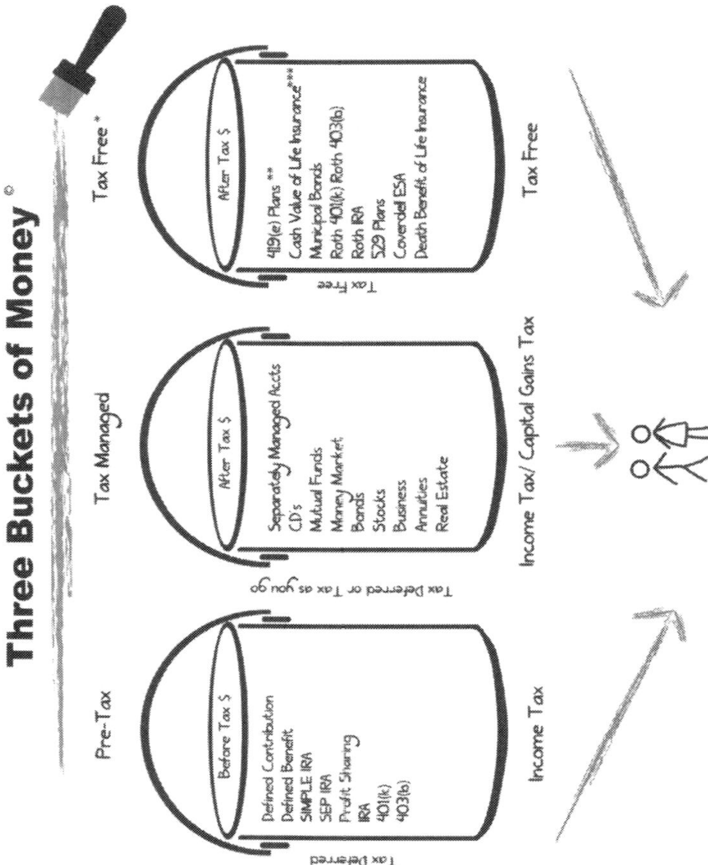

Chapter 3

The Three Tax Buckets

"We contend that for a nation to try to tax itself into prosperity is like a man standing in a bucket and trying to lift himself up by the handle."

~Winston Churchill

This training material has been prepared to assist our licensed financial professional and client's advisors. It is designed to provide general information in regard to the subject matter covered. It should be used with the understanding that Prudential is not rendering legal, accounting or tax advice. Such services should be provided by the clients own advisors.

*This bucket is potentially income tax free and under certain circumstances may lose their tax favored status.

** Prudential's sole role with regard to any 419(e) arrangement is that of a product provider. Prudential is not providing the 419 concept. Prudential shall not have any involvement, not even as a product provider only, with regard to the multi-employer 419A(f)(6) plans. Additionally, Prudential is neither endorsing the use of the 419 strategy nor the use of any 419 concept sponsor.

*** Cash value of Life Insurance will grow generally income tax free and can be accessed during lifetime income tax free utilizing loans and withdrawals up to basis assuming the policy is not a Modified Endowment Contract (MEC). However, if the policy is cash surrendered or lapses due to nonpayment of premiums during the insured's lifetime, ordinary income taxes must be paid on accumulated cash value above the cost basis of the policy. Death proceeds are typically income tax free. If the policy is a MEC, there may also be a 10% tax penalty for distributions prior to age 591/2.

At every stage of our life we are faced with paying taxes, whether we are earning, spending, or saving money. Taxes are so ingrained in our daily life; most people never pay attention to the total amount of taxes we pay during a year or even our lifetime. Typically, we become sharply aware of our income tax liability when we file our annual tax return. This prompts us to ask our accountant if there is anything else that we can do to reduce the bill. One of the most overlooked areas by financial advisors and clients is the impact taxes have on wealth accumulation. A person's net worth can be greatly enhanced with the right tax strategy or diminished by the wrong tax strategy. By employing a disciplined savings plan with the appropriate investment allocation based on your risk tolerance and the proper tax strategy, your financial security for retirement can be achieved. Let's take a look at how we can potentially reduce taxes over our lifetime.

The three buckets of money distinguishes how assets are taxed during the contribution, growth and income stages. There are three different tax structures in which assets are categorized. The three buckets will represent the three tax structures in which they are labeled the pre-tax bucket, tax managed bucket and tax free bucket. Each bucket has a unique tax strategy that can have flaws if not properly managed. My job is to help you uncover the hidden flaws and find money that may be falling through the cracks.

Pre-Tax Bucket

The pre-tax bucket allows you to invest money on a "before tax basis" giving you a tax deduction. The interest accumulation grows tax deferred until you withdraw funds at a future date. At retirement, withdrawals are income taxable at your income tax rate during retirement. The types of plans that go into this bucket are traditional IRA's, 401(k), profit sharing plans, 403(b), 457, SIMPLE IRA's, Simplified Employee Pension plans (SEP), defined contribution and defined benefit plans. Each plan has different contribution rules and plan rules. The one thing they have in common is the tax structure.

The advantages of the pre-tax bucket are saving taxes immediately when you make contributions into the plan and potentially being in a lower income tax bracket as you harvest the income at retirement. For example, a taxpayer in a 33% income tax bracket during the working years then harvests the income in a 28% tax bracket during retirement. The tax efficiency of this approach makes a lot of sense because the taxpayer saves 5%. Also, this strategy is beneficial if tax rates decrease in the future giving the investor even greater gains.

However, it would be wise to project your future retirement income streams to determine future tax liability. If you are in the same tax bracket or a higher tax bracket in the future, the tax outcome may not be as pleasant. For example, a young dentist client was maximizing his 401(k) plan in his practice on a pre-tax basis. I discovered he was paying a net effective tax rate of 7% (after deductions) due to tax write offs from his dental practice and personal deductions.

When I projected his future retirement income streams, he was in the maximum income tax bracket with few deductions. There was no tax advantage to this young dentist's savings plan. He was obtaining a modest tax deduction today to pay a sizable income tax bill in the future. "Sometimes it makes more sense to pay taxes on the seed versus the harvest." In this dentist's situation, he will pay taxes on the "harvest versus the seed" costing him substantial tax dollars. As the dentist's practice matures and income flourishes, considering a pre-tax approach to investing will be prudent. Until that time, investing in after tax investments such as a Roth 401(k) plan will produce greater results.

Those starting late with their savings plan for retirement may want to consider maximizing the pre-tax savings to accelerate your preparedness for retirement. For example, a self-employed oral surgeon had little set aside with less than 15 years until retirement. Due to a divorce, his retirement funds were eliminated. He had resigned to live a simple life retiring at age 70 with a $150,000 per year retirement budget. He was earning $700,000 per year in his business landing him in the maximum income tax bracket of 39.6%. He needed retirement savings fast. Who knows how long his health may last to perform his highly paid skill. In order to maximize his pre-tax savings, we established a defined benefit plan allowing him to defer over $200,000 per year. With this retirement savings approach, he was able to save the funds in a 39.6% marginal income tax bracket and harvest the income in a 28% marginal income tax bracket. This enabled him to meet his retirement goals in the most tax efficient manner.

Knowing when to change retirement savings strategies and which one to use should be discussed on a frequent basis with your financial planner. An owner of a small business was showing very little profit for several years as they were building their customer base. We implemented a 401(k) plan in his business giving him the option to either save on a pre-tax basis for the immediate tax benefit or save in a Roth option with after tax proceeds so he will have tax free retirement income. He started saving for retirement utilizing the Roth option due to his 15% marginal income tax rate. However, as his business flourished, I transitioned him to the pre-tax savings due to his 33% marginal income tax bracket. However, before we made the decision to change retirement savings tax strategies, a full assessment of his family's financial situation needed to be evaluated to ensure we were doing the right thing.

Three Buckets of Money °

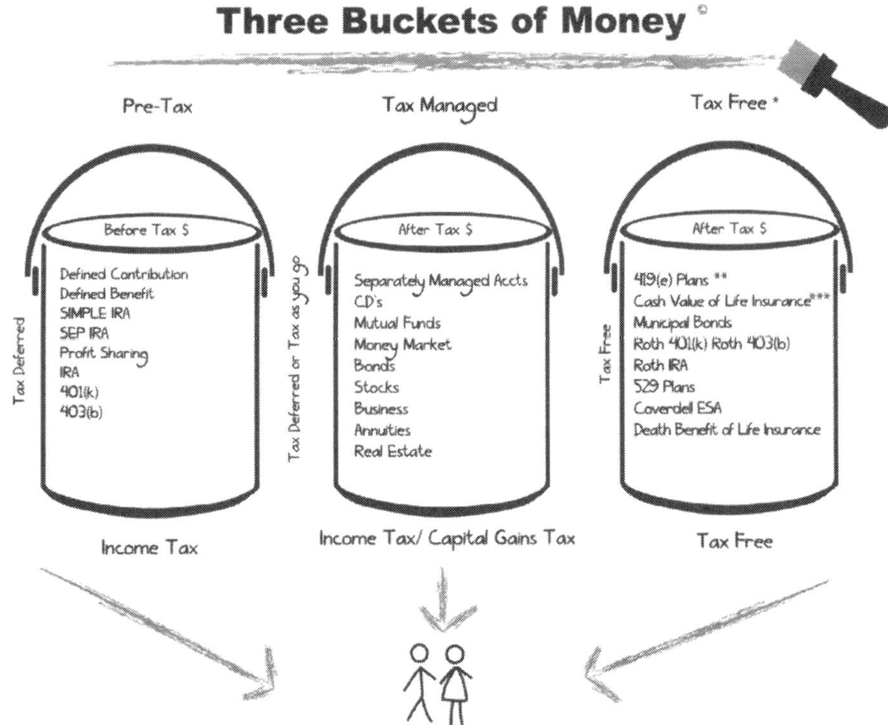

Tax Managed Bucket

The second bucket of money I call the tax managed due to the complexity of the tax issues based on the assets held in this bucket. This bucket can be tax efficient or very inefficient based on how you manage the assets within the bucket. The money invested in this bucket is after tax dollars. The money grows either tax deferred or you will pay taxes as you go. In the distribution years, you'll either pay taxes at your ordinary income tax rate or the long-term capital gains rate based upon the financial instrument in the bucket.

Within the bucket are assets such as individual stocks, bonds, mutual funds, exchange traded funds, certificates of deposit (CD), money market, savings accounts, non-qualified annuities, real estate, privately held business interests, alternatives, and separately managed accounts (SMA's). Often, assets in this bucket can be tax inefficient depending on your individual income tax brackets. Let's assume you are in a 39.6% federal income tax bracket with the 3.8% Obama care tax, a total of 43.4%. In addition, the state you live in levees a 5.8% state income tax on the investment earnings for a total of 49.2%. Let's assume you are invested in a mutual fund in which the money manager's turnover ratio is 100% (which is not uncommon). A turnover ratio is how often a money manager purchases and sells stocks within a 12 month period. With a 100% turnover ratio, all of the gains within the mutual fund will be taxed at the short-term capital gains rate (holding period less than 12 months) which is taxed at your ordinary income tax rate.

In this particular example, if you earned a 10% rate of return net of fees for the year, the net rate of return after taxes is 5.8%. It seems to me this investor is taking a lot of risk for such a modest rate of return net after taxes. By repositioning these assets in tax efficient mutual funds (low turnover ratios) or separately managed accounts with a tax mandate, or a non-qualified tax deferred annuity, you can recapture a good portion of your return.

For those who are unfamiliar with separately managed accounts (SMA's), the investment minimums are often $100,000. The SMA's are transparent in which you own the individual stocks or bonds in the portfolio with a money manager managing the portfolio for you. Compare that to a mutual fund, where you own common shares in the mutual fund not aware of the trading activity of the fund manager or the securities owned in your fund because of daily changes. A mutual fund's semi- annual report must disclose the securities owned at the end of a period of time, but it can change rapidly. In addition, you can place restrictions on the manager not to purchase specific stocks or industries.

If you don't want to own tobacco stocks in the portfolio because of the negative health effects, you can exclude them. The tax benefits of a SMA are that you can place a tax mandate on the money manager in which the money manager must own stocks for 12 months and 1 day to capture the long-term capital gains status. The manager can tax harvest the losses in the portfolio each year so you can write a portion off on your income tax return or offset capital gains in the portfolio thereby enhancing your net rate of return on your investments.

Higher income taxpayers can greatly benefit with SMA's as a part of their retirement portfolio. As you can see with the tax managed bucket, being tax conscious can pay big dividends to investors in all income tax brackets.

When evaluating mutual funds be aware of the turnover ratio of each fund. High turnover ratios means gains will be taxed at ordinary income tax rates versus the lower long-term capital gains rates. For example, an actively managed large cap value portfolio that concentrates on dividend paying stocks may have a buy and hold mandate as long as the dividend growth rate of the fund meets their criteria. The low turnover fund will have a dividend distribution each year taxed at the lower, long-term capital gains rates. By transitioning to tax efficient mutual funds, you can lower your tax bill thereby enhancing your net rate of return on investment. In addition, I've seen very little difference in long-term performance of high versus low turnover funds over long periods of time.

Non-qualified annuities are an excellent tax deferral strategy allowing your income and capital appreciation from the sub accounts to compound over time. Non-qualified means that after tax contributions are made into an investment account. With an annuity, the interest and growth are tax deferred until you begin making withdrawals.

Distributions from a non-qualified annuity are required at age 95 versus age 70 ½ such as with qualified investments like a traditional IRA. If the investment is accessed prior to age 59 ½, income taxes will be due on the growth of the investment with a 10% tax penalty imposed. The principal will be free of taxes and penalties. The advantage of an annuity is the compounded tax deferred growth which can help minimize your tax bill each and every year you allow the investment to grow. Also, if you are in a lower income tax bracket during retirement than you were in your working years, the non-qualified annuity works to your benefit when accessing funds for retirement.

To help you understand the power of tax deferral on investment accounts consider the Rule of 72. The rule of 72 is a time-honored maxim that speaks to the power of compound interest on long-term investments. Simply stated, if you take your interest rate and divide it into 72, it will tell you how long it will take to double your money. For example, if you invested $100,000 and received a 7% return net after fees and taxes on your investment, it will take 10 years for your money to reach $200,000.

Conversely, consider how long it will take your money to double in a taxable account if you are in a 25% tax bracket and 39.6% tax bracket. You will need to apply the rule of 96 and the rule of 120 to estimate how long it will take for your investment to double using these different tax rates. The Rule of 96 accounts for a 25% income tax rate and using the above example, it will take 14 years before your money will double (reach $200,000). With the Rule of 120 accounting for a 39.6% annual tax rate, it will take 17 years for your money to double.

Let's assume for a moment that Investor A and Investor B are age 35 paying 25% in annual taxes with a 30 year time horizon before entering retirement. Each investor has $100,000 in an investment account earning 7% rate of return. Investor A invests in a taxable account and Investor B invests in a tax deferred account. What is the impact of tax deferral over 30 years?

Investor A will double money every 14 years allowing the investor to double twice during that timeframe leaving an account value just over $400,000. Investor B will double money every 10 years allowing the investor to double the account three times giving a portfolio value of $800,000. Let's assume these investors are in a 39.6% tax bracket as the investments accumulate.

Investor A will only be able to double one time with an account value less than $400,000. Investor B will have an after tax account value of more than $500,000. The power of tax deferral can be a game changer for those preparing for retirement with non-qualified assets.

Certain asset classes can provide greater tax benefits than other asset classes. Typically bond income is taxed at ordinary income tax rates. However, by positioning the bonds in an annuity, IRA or other tax deferred account, you can wait to pay taxes in the future when you may be in lower tax rates. Also, asset classes that generate significant short-term capital gains, such as high- turnover stock mutual funds or SMA's, can benefit from being in a tax deferred account. Paying attention to what you are investing in is very important in becoming tax efficient.

Some investors will trade tax efficiency for liquidity of their investments especially if you are younger than age 59 ½. In this situation, dividend paying stocks, low-turnover mutual funds and tax-efficient funds should be sought after. For example, with a dividend paying stock, you achieve tax deferral through the appreciation of the stock while paying taxes on the qualified dividends generated each year at the long-term capital gains rates. If you are in the 10% and 15% income tax brackets, your tax rate is 0% on dividends.

If you are in the 25% tax rate up to the 35% tax rate, you will pay 15% on dividends and capital gains (and possibly the 3.8% Obamacare tax) and if you are in the 39.6% income tax rate, you will pay 20% plus an additional 3.8% Obama care tax.

Depending on your tax bracket, you can minimize the tax impact with dividend payers.

There are several asset classes that are very tax inefficient such as high-yield bonds, REITs, core bond funds, cash and cash equivalents. During your working years, you may just have to pay taxes on the growth of these funds to maintain a balanced portfolio for your liquidity needs.

Often these assets are used for emergency purposes and shorter-term goals during your household formation stage. However, when you enter into retirement after age 59 ½, you can shift these assets into more tax efficient investments such as no load non-qualified annuities or exchange your emergency fund from your taxable account into Roth IRA's eliminating all income taxation.

This is not a complete discussion of how to manage the tax managed bucket, but it will give you a sample of things you can do to be more tax efficient. It's important that you work with a competent advisor that can help you manage your way through the tax maize.

Three Buckets of Money ©

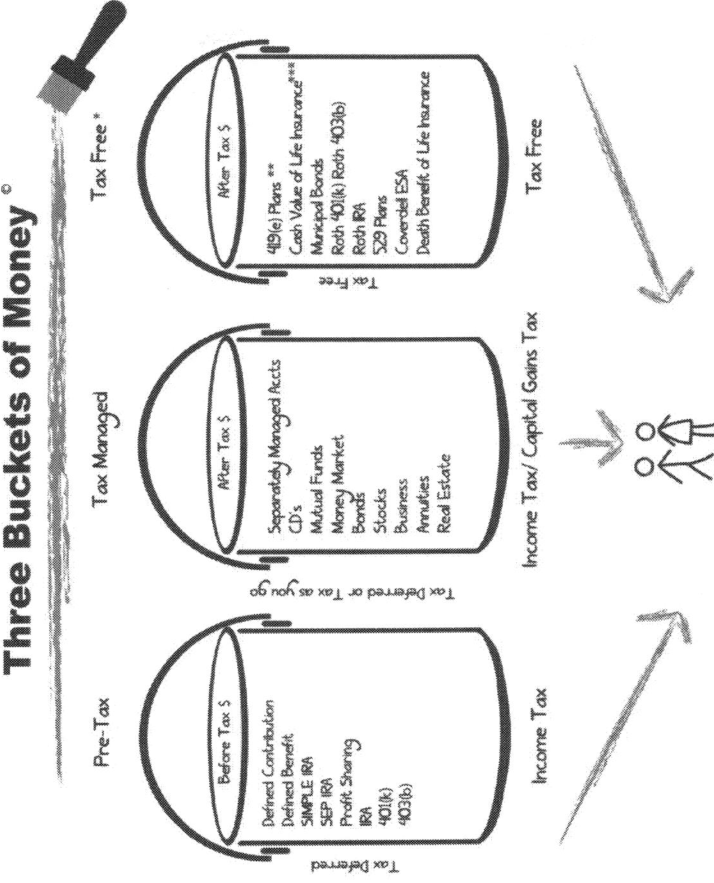

Tax Free Bucket

The third bucket is called the 'Tax Free Bucket.' This bucket is probably the most underutilized and most tax efficient structure for ordinary people. In the tax free bucket, you are depositing after tax dollars into the bucket with the assets growing income tax free and can be withdrawn income tax free as long as you comply with the specific plan rules. The plan types for retirement in this bucket are Roth IRA, Roth 401(k) Roth 403(b) and 419(e) plans. In addition, *life insurance cash values and municipal bonds may provide tax fee benefits. For educational purposes, plan types are Coverdell educational savings accounts and 529 plans.

The primary benefit of the 'Tax Free Bucket' is that income from your investments for college and retirement are tax free. During retirement, if you have $50,000 of income coming from this bucket it will translate into $50,000 of spending money. The education savings vehicles must be used for qualified education expenses in order to be tax free. This is where a dollar doesn't necessarily equal a dollar when compared to taxable income from other investments.

Stated another way, let's assume you need an income of $100,000 per year. If the income is from the pre-tax and the tax managed bucket (assuming little tax planning has been completed and the funds are taxed at ordinary income tax rates), all your income is taxable.

Assuming 30% in federal and state income taxes, you will have $70,000 of spending money. If the assets come from the tax free bucket, you have $100,000 of spending money. Which would you rather have? Crazy question, right! You would want the $100,000 tax free income.

*cash values are accessed through loans and withdrawals. Assuming the policy is not a Modified Endowment Contract (MEC), withdrawals up to basis can be taken tax free and then loans, which are not taxable as long as the policy does not terminate prior to death. Distributions from MECs receive less favorable tax treatment.

Tax Diversification

In addition, the income from the tax free bucket can help lower your income tax bracket from other income sources in retirement. In the previous example, what if $50,000 came from the pre-tax bucket and $50,000 came from the tax free bucket? The tax free income will lower the federal tax rate from 28% to 15% on the pre-tax bucket's income distribution. Let's say you were in a 28% federal income tax bracket during your working years thereby reducing your tax bracket to 13% in retirement. The 16% difference in taxes could make a substantial difference in your retirement lifestyle. In addition, if tax rates increase in the future, you will have locked in your tax rate with the tax free bucket at zero and helped minimize the tax impact due to the increased tax rates.

Going back to our example, $50,000 is taxed at 15% giving you $42,500 net after taxes with the remainder being tax free at $50,000. Your spending money is now $92,500. By tax diversifying your investments, you can lower your future income tax liability on retirement income giving you a better lifestyle during your golden years.

The bottom line is that the assets in the tax free bucket help lower the income tax rates on taxable investments providing you with a tax efficient retirement. If you have no assets in the tax free bucket, you will have no tax control during your retirement years.

Furthermore, by having assets diversified appropriately in all three buckets, you will have flexibility if tax laws change that could detrimentally affect one of the buckets. Stay in control of your retirement by tax diversifying your retirement savings.

Chapter 4

Tax Free Retirement

"Genius is 1 percent inspiration and 99 percent perspiration."

~Thomas A. Edison

Attempting a tax free retirement or a tax efficient retirement can often be created by utilizing the combination of all three buckets. The income distributions must be measured appropriately from each bucket to maximize the tax efficiency. Income sources will be taxed differently based on how the assets were saved in the accumulation stage. By mixing and matching the income streams appropriately, you can achieve a very tax efficient retirement income distribution and may even accomplish a tax free retirement.

Income sources for retirement are typically investment income, social security, annuities and pensions. Few people have pensions today so I'm leaving this income source out of this example. Assets can be located in multiple buckets, but the composition of these assets must be located in the right position in order to achieve a virtually federal income tax free retirement. Let's take a look at an example of how this may work. Your income objective for retirement is $100,000. You have assets in the pre-tax bucket and the tax free buckets. Both, you and your spouse are age 66 taking your full retirement benefit which pays $20,000 each from the social security administration. An income stream of $22,700 is coming from a traditional IRA. Also, you are pulling out $37,300 from Roth IRA's and cash value life insurance. Under the current tax rules, the $100,000 from these sources is federally income tax free. You may be asking yourself, how can you take income from the pre-tax bucket, tax free?

Under the current income tax law, you have standard deductions and personal exemptions for a married couple filing a joint income tax return that totals $22,700. Also, you may have itemized deductions in addition that can offset income tax liability. You match up the income with the tax write offs.

Secondly, most people think social security benefits are tax free. This is not true! Social security benefits are tax free if your modified adjusted income is less than $32,000 for a married couple filing jointly. If your modified adjusted gross income is over $32,000 but does not exceed $44,000, 50% of your social security benefits are subject to ordinary income tax. If your modified adjusted gross income is $44,000 or over, 85% of your social security benefits are taxed. In this situation, the modified adjusted gross income doesn't exceed the threshold.

You may be wondering, "what about the Roth and cash value life insurance income from the tax free bucket?" Roth income and cash value life insurance income is not included in the calculation for modified adjusted gross income rules. You could have $1,000,000 per year of income from these sources and it would not be included. The included income sources are one half of the social security benefits and the traditional IRA income which was zeroed out due to personal exemptions and standard deductions. Therefore, there is no federal income tax in this particular example.

The Tax Efficient Retirement

Traditional IRA Income → **Offset by** → Personal Exemptions. Itemized deductions and/or standard deductions

Social Security → **Tax Free if** → MAGI is less than threshold

ROTH IRA, ROTH 401K ROTH 403B and Cash Value Life Insurance Income → **Tax Free** → Income Excluded from MAGI rule

The Tax Efficient Retirement

In the diagram, you can see that traditional IRA income is offset by personal exemptions, standard deductions and itemized deductions. Social security is tax free as long as you are below the social security threshold. Then, of course, Roth income and cash value life insurance is excluded from the modified adjusted gross income rule. By strategically allocating the income from the assets in an appropriate manner, you can substantially lower your income taxes going into your retirement years thereby enhancing your lifestyle.

There are multiple ways to become more tax efficient with investment assets even if your situation is not perfect as in the previous example. However, I do not want to overwhelm you in this book. It is my intention to help you understand the concept of tax efficiency and how it can play a major role in providing for your retirement security. Tax efficiency is a key focus in retirement planning.

Tax Impact on Your Savings

# Years	(No Tax) $ 1.00 Doubled	(Taxed) $1.00 doubled
1	2	1.72
2	4	2.96
3	8	5.09
4	16	8.75
5	32	15.05
6	64	25.89
7	128	44.53
8	256	76.60
9	512	131.75
10	1,024	226.61
11	2,048	389.77
12	4,096	670.41
13	8,192	1,153.11
14	16,384	1,983.34
15	32,768	3,411.35
16	65,536	5,867.53
17	131,072	10,092.15
18	262,144	17,358.49
19	524,288	29,856.61
20	1,048,576	51,353.37

The Tax Impact on Your Savings

As we take a look at the diagram above, this is an over exaggeration of the tax impact on investments, but it does prove a point that you must be tax wise. Assume for a moment that you gave me a one dollar bill and every year for the next 20 years I doubled your money. So, $1.00 is doubled to $2.00 and etc. for 20 years. At the end of 20 years, your account balance is $1,048,576.

If this investment is invested in the tax free bucket, you will have $1,048,576 of tax free spending money. However, if the assets are in the pre-tax bucket, the assets would grow tax deferred for 20 years until you take distribution of the assets.

Assuming you are in a 28% tax bracket, the asset value will decrease to $754,974 after taxes. Now you have $754,974 of spending money. If your income tax bracket was as high as the 39.6% plus 3.8% for Obama care, your tax free spending money will be reduced to $593,494. As you can see, the government is taxing financial success.

What if we invested the $1.00 doubled it to $2.00 and paid taxes on the growth each year? So your $2.00 will be reduced to $1.72 due to the 28% tax. Then, you doubled the $1.72 and netted $2.96. If you do this process for 20 years, the investment is reduced to a measly $51,353. You lost almost $1,000,000 dollars due to taxes. This approach is invested in the tax managed bucket where you pay taxes as you go each and every year. I find this savings approach very common with self-directed brokerage accounts where the investor owns mutual funds with high turnover ratios.

To recap the tax impact of this example, the tax free bucket has $1,048,576, the pre-tax bucket has $754,974 net after taxes and the tax managed bucket has a whopping $51,353. Which bucket would you rather have your money in during retirement? My preference is in the tax free bucket!

I realize this is an overdramatic example of the impact of taxes on your investments; however, there is a great deal of truth in this example. The more tax efficient we become with our assets, the more money you will have for the retirement years. Many of you are behind on retirement savings as it is, you surely don't want to get further behind due to being tax inefficient with your investment savings.

I find that individuals start building a retirement income plan when they approach retirement versus at the beginning of their careers. As you can see, the optimal time to work on your retirement income strategy is during the planting season versus the harvest season. When assets are placed in tax inefficient locations, it can be difficult to reallocate the assets in tax efficient investments. However, I'm finding there are options for individuals at any age to become more tax efficient with their retirement income, even if you are in retirement. You must be willing to look at alternative strategies for your investments which may be very different from the way you accumulated your wealth.

Chapter 5

Filling Up the Tax Free Bucket

"The hardest thing in the world to understand is
the income tax."

~Albert Einstein

There are numerous opportunities for maximizing your tax free bucket in preparation for retirement. Often, you can reposition assets from the pre-tax bucket and the tax managed bucket to obtain a superior income tax result during your retirement years. Repositioning assets that are taxable into a tax free retirement income stream can lower the income tax burden on taxable investments such as traditional IRA's, rental real estate, pension income, taxable investments and your social security benefits. Also, you can lower your premiums for Medicare as well. As you read further, I'm presenting some ideas on how to maximize your tax free bucket. However, please consult with your tax advisor before trying to do this on your own.

The ideas presented in this chapter are technical in nature. Skip this chapter if you are a big picture person so you won't get bogged down in the detail Roth IRA, 403(b) and 401(k) plans

As we discussed earlier, the tax free bucket allows you to contribute after tax dollars into the bucket. The investment grows tax free and it can be distributed tax free, as long as you follow government guidelines. One of the most popular tools for tax free retirement income is the Roth (IRA, 401(k) or 403(b)).

Let's take a look at how the Roth (IRA, 401(k) or 403(b)) can be one of your biggest allies in reducing taxes in the future. Almost everyone can make contributions to a Roth IRA every year even if you are a very high wage earner. For 2015, you will be eligible to make a $5,500 contribution and if you are age 50 and over an additional $1,000 contribution. You can make this contribution for husband and wife even if there is a non-working spouse in the household as long as there is sufficient earned income. If discretionary income is not available, consider repositioning assets from the tax managed bucket (such as non- qualified brokerage accounts, savings accounts, certificates of deposit, etc.). You are literally moving funds from a taxable pocket to a tax free pocket. If you are concerned about the lack of liquidity of the investment in emergencies, Roth IRA rules will allow you to withdraw your principal prior to age 59 1/2 without consequences. The interest will need to stay in the Roth until you are age 59 1/2 to bypass income tax and penalties.

For those high wage earners phased out of making Roth IRA contribution, you can make after tax traditional IRA contributions and convert the traditional IRA to a Roth IRA. You will pay income taxes on the interest generated from the time of deposit to the time of conversion. However, please be aware of the pro-rata rules of IRA's when doing a conversion. This idea could be a tax nightmare if completed incorrectly and you also had pre-tax IRA contributions. Also, the pro-rata rules do not aggregate your spouse's IRAs with yours. If you are unable to use the nondeductible IRA contributions with immediate conversion approach to an IRA that does not mean your spouse can't contribute. Roth 401(k) plans are becoming more popular with employers today than in previous years.

The maximum contribution for 2015 in a Roth is $18,000 with a catch up provision for those 50 years and older of $6,000 totaling a maximum contribution of $24,000. In addition, if you are under the income limit for exempting out in a Roth contribution, you can make an additional Roth IRA contribution. If you are 50 years old you can double up and make a total of $30,500 Roth 401(k) and Roth IRA contribution. If you are over the income limitation rule, remember you can make an after tax IRA contribution and convert to a Roth IRA for you and your spouse. If both husband and wife have access to a Roth 401(k) plan and Roth IRA, a total of $61,000 per year can be invested. By paying attention to these rules, you can make significant Roth contributions on a yearly basis.

For young investors starting their careers maximizing Roth IRA, 403(b), 401(k) should be the tax structure of choice due to being in the lowest tax bracket of their lifetime. The potential for your lifetime earnings to increase is significant causing you to be in higher income tax brackets as your career progresses. Paying taxes on the seed versus the harvest will enable you to have a more secure and flexible retirement. As you approach the higher income tax brackets, you can switch from making Roth contributions to pre-tax contributions. By managing tax brackets, you can save yourself significant tax dollars. For those individuals who aspire to retire early, having the ability to withdraw your principal from the Roth IRA without any tax consequences prior to age 59 1/2 will give you added flexibility. Remember, you must always begin with the end in mind when plotting out your tax strategy and your financial goals.

For middle and low income earners, Roth contributions may be preferable due to being in very low tax brackets. Your contributions to a pre- tax IRA may receive very little to no income tax deduction benefits due to income level, standard deductions, personal exemptions and itemized income tax deductions. By making Roth contributions versus pre-tax contributions, the Roth income at retirement may help you avoid taxation on your social security benefits, taxable income and decrease Medicare premiums.

High wage earners should consider Roth contributions if their projected retirement income is estimated to be the same or in a higher tax bracket during retirement. This will provide a risk hedge in your tax plan in case federal and state governments increase income tax rates in the future. However, this bet may work against you if tax rates go down in the future.

If you work for a company that allows you to make after tax contributions into a 401(k) plan, the Internal Revenue Service (IRS) has given new guidance on converting the after tax contributions to a Roth tax free within your plan. The IRS also stated that the after tax dollars can be transferred out of your plan and converted to a self-directed Roth IRA. In addition, you can convert pre-tax 401(k) contributions to a Roth inside your plan bypassing the IRA pro rata rules. However, all of this hinges on the plan administrator of the 401(k) plan allowing these conversions.

The pro rata rules warrant a discussion to help you avoid a major tax mess. When converting after tax contributions of a traditional IRA to a Roth IRA, only a portion of the conversion maybe tax free.

To calculate the tax free portion, you must include all traditional IRA's, SIMPLE IRA's, and SEP IRA's as of December 31st of the year in which you make your conversion. Then, you calculate the ratio of the total after tax contributions to the total balances of the IRA's which gives you the pro rata amount that is not taxed. If you want to make partial conversions of your traditional IRA's and the pro rata rules apply to your situation, you can transfer all or a portion of your traditional IRA into your 401(k) plan and complete the Roth conversions inside the 401(k) plan. If you are age 59 1/2 with an in service distribution option in your employer sponsored 401(k) plan, you can transfer the 401(k) assets to a self-directed IRA giving you more investment control.

When considering Roth conversions, monitoring tax brackets and strategically converting only portions of your qualified plan assets (eq. IRA) will save you money. Let's assume the taxpayer is in the 25% tax bracket and can earn an additional $50,000 that year before reaching the 28% tax bracket. The $200,000 pre-tax retirement account should be converted over several years versus in one tax year. The one time conversion could send the taxpayer's marginal income tax rate as high as 33%. Converting $50,000 per year for 4 years will save tax money allowing the taxpayer to maintain the 25% tax rate for the entire conversion.

Roth monies are a preferable asset to leave as an inheritance for your spouse, children and/or grandchildren. Roth assets are passed to heir's income tax free. However, they are calculated in your assets for estate tax purposes. Furthermore, there are no required minimum distribution rules while you are alive requiring you to take an income at age 70 ½.

For those that do not need the income from their Roth IRA, you can continue growing the asset tax free to provide as an inheritance for heirs. Moving the assets downstream is called "stretching your IRA."

At the Roth owner's death, the IRA can be paid out in a lump sum to the beneficiary, transferred to an inherited IRA with a 5 year time limit to taking full distribution or transferred to an inherited IRA that distributes income each year based on the beneficiary's life expectancy. By stretching the IRA over the beneficiary's life expectancy, the funds can continue to grow tax free.

For example, let's assume that the required minimum distribution for the beneficiary is 2% of the December 31st account balance. But, the investment return on the Roth is 8% for the year thereby allowing the account to grow by 6%. With good investment performance, the Roth IRA can grow into a substantial tax free asset for your heirs potentially providing tax free income for their entire lifetime. In addition, if your heirs need to take a distribution that exceeds the required minimum distribution, they can access the entire account without tax penalty at any age. Lastly, as the spouse of a deceased Roth IRA owner, he/she can roll over the IRA into their name and begin taking tax free income distributions as early as age 59 1/2.

When converting a traditional IRA to a Roth IRA, you should have funds outside of the IRA to pay the tax bill. I find most people do not have the money to pay the taxes for the conversion or are not willing to give up their liquidity to complete a conversion.

A very effective way to convert pre-tax IRA monies to Roth is acquiring life insurance on the IRA owner for the amount of the tax with anticipation that the surviving spouse converts the account at the IRA owner's death.

The life insurance will be paid tax free to the spouse and provide the funds to pay the tax bill.

Of course, the beneficiary could die first and the conversion plan is thwarted unless there is life insurance on the beneficiary. Even if there is no life insurance on the beneficiary, the heirs will receive an enhanced estate from the deceased IRA owner's life insurance.

Business owners will often post losses on their tax return due to losses associated with their business. You can utilize the losses by converting your traditional IRA into a Roth IRA creating a tax free conversion. Carryover losses from previous tax years can also be utilized for Roth conversions. Be aware of tax loss conversions as you sit down with your financial advisor each year. Tax loss conversions are great opportunities to turn taxable investments into tax free investments.

When terminating a life insurance policy where the cost basis (premiums paid into the policy) exceeds the cash surrender value of the policy, there is no tax loss that can be written off on your income taxes in the event the policy lapses or is cash surrendered. However, a non-qualified annuity with a cost basis higher than the surrender value may be a tax write off. The tax code will allow you to 1035 exchange a life insurance policy into an annuity.

After the funds have been invested in the annuity for 6 months, you can cash surrender the annuity and may be able to capitalize on the loss. You will want to consider a no load annuity if you plan on utilizing this technique due to surrender charges imposed by most annuity contracts. Then, you can convert the traditional IRA to a Roth IRA capitalizing on the tax loss.

Note it is not a dollar for dollar benefit since the loss on the annuity is treated as an itemized deduction in the category of miscellaneous loss subject to a 2% floor.

For those retiring with a Roth 401(k) plan, make certain you have a Roth IRA plan that was established for 5 years prior to your retirement. When rolling over Roth 401(k) assets into a Roth IRA, the 5 year rule applies to the Roth IRA separately from the Roth 401(k). You must be age 59 1/2 and have established a Roth IRA for 5 tax years before withdrawals are income tax free.

Investing for years in the Roth 401(k) doesn't satisfy the 5 year rule for Roth IRA's. This could be a problem in your retirement plan if proper planning hasn't been achieved. A key point here is to establish a Roth IRA at least 5 years before rolling over your Roth 401(k) plan assets this gives you immediate access to the investment growth free from income taxes.

For those self-employed with children, consider employing the kids in the business. The kids can earn $6,500 per year in 2017 without incurring federal income taxes. Also, as long as they are a minor, you do not have to withhold social security taxes and Medicare taxes. The funds can be invested into a Roth IRA due to the child having employment income. The principal can be withdrawn without penalties or taxes to be utilized for college, down payment on a house or to start a business. Of course, keeping the funds designated for retirement will reap great benefits for them with 40 to 50 years of compound growth on the investments. As long as a child has employment income, anyone can make the Roth contribution for them, even a grandparent. Please take note that for this to work there must be a valid job for the child to perform.

The following chart contrasts making a pre-tax IRA contribution versus an after Roth IRA contribution. Let's assume you make a $1,000 onetime contribution into a pre-tax investment such as a traditional IRA and a $750 after tax contribution into a Roth IRA assuming a 25% tax rate. The pretax investment grows to $5,743, assuming a 6% rate of return, while the tax free Roth investment grows to $4,308. If tax rates stay the same in retirement, the after tax investment value is exactly the same due to paying 25% tax on the pre-tax contribution. If your tax brackets never change during your life, the answer is that it doesn't matter. You will get the same result in either tax strategy.

However, the tipping point would be if social security benefits will be taxed or not-taxed based on the chosen tax structure. If tax rates go down in the future, the pre-tax bucket is a much better strategy. If the tax rates go up in the future, the Roth is a better investment strategy. Trying to project retirement income streams with a comprehensive financial plan will help you make wise decisions on which strategy to invest.

	Pre Tax	Roth
Tax Rate = 25% Contribution	$1,000	$750
Account Value in 30 years @ 6%	$5,743	$4,308
Tax Rate Stays the Same After Tax Account Value in 30 years	$4,308	$4,308
Tax Rates Go DOWN in Retirement Tax Rate = 15% After Tax Account Value in 30 years	$4,882	$4,308
Tax Rates Go UP in Retirement Tax Rate = 28% After Tax Account Value in 30 years	$4,135	$4,308

Life Insurance as a Tax Free Asset Class

Life insurance cash values are tax favored if the policy is structured appropriately. The cash values of a life insurance policy can be utilized to supplement retirement, pay for college, and provide for emergencies. The cash value of the policy will grow tax free and can be accessed tax free as long as you withdraw the basis (premiums deposited) and take a loan against the cash values in the policy. The loans reduce the cash value as well as the accrued death benefits so that at death the loan is paid off. The death benefit is income tax free when paid out to beneficiaries. However, if you cash surrender a life insurance policy, you will pay ordinary income taxes on the difference between your cost basis and accrued cash value (unreduced by the loan balance). So it's very important that you die with a life insurance contract that makes the most of all its tax free benefits. Types of cash value accumulation products are whole life, variable universal life, indexed universal life and cash accumulation universal life.

With cash value accumulation universal life policies, there is a minimum premium and a maximum premium that can be contributed. The minimum premium is necessary to maintain the policy until death. Adding additional premiums will allow you to accumulate cash value tax favored for wealth accumulation needs. The maximum premium is determined by a formula which is based on the amount of death benefit, age and gender. The maximum premium can be significantly higher than the minimum premium each year. However, if you deposit more premiums than the IRS allows, the contract will become a modified endowment contract causing the taxable gain to be considered distributed first and also causes loans to be income taxable.

Following the IRS rules is very important to maintain the tax favored benefits. All of this sounds really complicated; however, insurance companies monitor these contracts each year to make certain these rules are not violated. If you violate the rules, the IRS will give you a short window of time to fix it.

To supplement your retirement income tax free by utilizing the cash values in the life insurance policy, you must take a withdrawal of your basis (premium deposits) and policy loans. Insurance companies today have very favorable policy loans and at death are paid off through a reduction in the death benefit. The insured can take a systematic monthly income stream from the policy as long as there is sufficient cash value to support the life insurance death benefit and income stream. Obtaining periodic ledgers projecting the policy's cash values and death benefits will be important in monitoring the policy's performance.

Sometimes the tax leverage of a life insurance policy can be greatly enhanced. Let's take a look at an example on how this has worked. I had a client who had an insurable interest on his mom and purchased $500,000 of death benefit. The son was the premium payer and beneficiary of the policy while funding it at the minimum premium. At the same time, he had a policy on his life funding it at minimum premium and naming his wife and children as beneficiaries. Several years later the mom died paying out the tax free death benefit to her son. The son then deposited the $500,000 into his life insurance policy where the cash values are growing income tax free and can be accessed income tax free during his lifetime utilizing loans/withdrawals. This transaction did not violate the modified endowment rules mentioned above.

For example, in this situation his minimum premium on his life was $10,000 per year and maximum premium was $50,000 per year. Each passing year the $40,000 extra that could have been deposited accrued until he utilized it at a later date. In year 13, the son could potentially deposit $520,000 in a lump sum to make up for the years in which he did not make the maximum premium payments.

The tax leverage is significant as the tax free death benefit was passed to her son. In turn, he deposits the funds in his life insurance policy allowing the money to grow income tax free until retirement when he plans on receiving a tax free income stream from the policy for the rest of his life at retirement. At his death, the death benefit will be paid out tax free to his heirs leaving a legacy to his wife and children. The tax leverage is significant in this situation. However, with a life insurance policy there must be a need for the life insurance before a carrier will provide the coverage. This is called an insurable interest.

Life Insurance (Tax Free) Death Benefit

Life insurance is an asset class of its own. Most people don't think of life insurance as being an asset class. However, this tool provides tremendous versatility as both a wealth accumulation and wealth transfer asset in retirement and estate planning. The life insurance will guarantee a death benefit which provides a secure financial base that gives an investor more comfort in taking additional investment risk with other financial assets. Life insurance can ensure financial security for your spouse and provide a legacy for children and grandchildren. In second marriages, life insurance may be useful in providing for a surviving spouse while leaving assets to your children from a previous marriage. In wealthy families, life insurance may enable equality in estates with illiquid family businesses; there may be a child that works in the business and others who do not. Also, it may be used to pay for estate taxes that are due nine months after the last spouse's death.

With asset values, most change over time with some increasing and some declining in value. In 2008, most individuals saw significant decline in real estate, stock, bond and alternatives. Traditional life insurance has attributes that smooth out your different asset class mixtures while living or at death. Life insurance has a predicable value where other asset classes are unknown. You simply don't know what the future value of a stock, bond, real estate or alternative investment. Life insurance costs can be guaranteed in no-lapse policies fixing the premium amount for a lifetime. Also, with no- lapse guaranteed life insurance the future value is not linked to market performance giving you peace of mind when markets decline. The tax benefits of the cash value have been mentioned above.

The beauty of using the benefits of life insurance while living is the income tax benefits. There is no federal, no state nor 3.8% Medicare surtax imposed on the lifetime growth of the cash value in the policy. With variable life contracts, you can rebalance your mutual fund portfolio (sub accounts) without incurring income taxes. You can also reallocate the portfolio completely without incurring tax liability.

Life insurance is very liquid at death and is not reduced by commissions or fees. The benefit is paid out very timely after death. Assets, such as businesses or real estate are hard to convert to cash in a timely manner at death. Also, the premiums paid for the death benefit provide significant leverage through life expectancy creating a favorable internal rate of return on the premiums when compared to other assets.

Furthermore, life insurance is easily divisible between beneficiaries and it allows multiple beneficiaries. Within several states, life insurance is asset protected for the owner and beneficiaries. Irrevocable life insurance trust owned policies are protected from the grantors and beneficiaries creditors based on the spendthrift provisions held in the trust document. In addition, the death benefit avoids probate and the claims of a descendant's creditors at death due to paying the proceeds to a designated beneficiary.

Life insurance will avoid the transfer tax if owned by an irrevocable life insurance trust. The death proceeds are immediately excluded from your estate which will avoid federal and state estate taxes. The generation skipping transfer tax and may not be subject to the generation skipping transfer tax (GST) if the premiums were allocated to the GST exemption.

If you transfer an existing life insurance into an irrevocable trust, you must wait three years from the date of transfer before it's removed completely from the estate. If the trustee purchases the policy and the trust owns it from the initial setup, it's immediately out of the estate for tax purposes.

Municipal Bonds

Municipal bonds, in the state of your residency are triple tax exempt which means there is no federal, state nor local taxes on the interest accrued. If you purchase a bond that is not in your state of residency, the bond may only be federal tax exempt. Where cash value of life insurance and Roth accounts are not included in your modified adjusted income to determine social security taxation and Medicare premiums, municipal bond interest is included in the calculation. Be aware of this rule when working through your tax planning during retirement. There may also be Alternative Minimum Tax consequences. Also note that while the interest on a municipal bond is income tax free, gain on the sale of the bond is not.

Immediate Annuities

An immediate annuity is best described as a pension plan for life if structured appropriately. Some immediate annuities only pay out for a specific period of time. An investor contributes after tax dollars into the immediate annuity which results in a tax exclusion on the portion of annuity payment that represents the principal deposited. The portion attributable to interest or earnings is income taxable. For example, a 70 year old couple may have a 60% tax exclusion from their retirement income by repositioning assets into an immediate annuity. Having a portion of your income coming in tax free can help lower income tax brackets, eliminate or reduce social security from being taxed and may lower Medicare premiums.

419 (e) Plans

Many people have never heard of 419 (e) plans. A 419 (e) plan is designed for small employers to set funds aside pre-tax to grow tax free and to be distributed tax free for health care benefits during your retirement years.

The funds can be utilized for health insurance premiums, Medicare premiums, medications, over the counter medical supplies and medications and any other out of pockets costs for health care.

Chapter 6

Social Security, a Tax Strategy?

"This law represents a cornerstone in a structure which is being built but is by no means completed—a structure intended to lessen the force of possible future depressions, to act as a protection to future administrations of the Government against the necessity of going deeply into debt to furnish relief to the needy—a law to flatten out the peaks and valleys of deflation and of inflation—in other words, a law that will take care of human needs and at the same time provide for the United States an economic structure of vastly greater soundness."

– August 14, 1935, Franklin Delano Roosevelt

For most Americans, social security benefits are a major source of retirement income. It is important to take into consideration how and when to start your social security income. There are consequences to taking the benefits before your full retirement age. By taking the benefits early (age 62), this will result in a reduced benefit for your entire life as well as a reduced survivor benefit for your spouse. This can have negative consequences especially for women since they have a much longer life expectancy than men. According to the Center of Retirement Research at Boston College, 90% of men take their Social Security Benefits before full retirement age thereby receiving a reduced personal and spousal benefit for life. In fact, the Social Security

Administration states that 63% of women receive a spousal benefit based off their husband's work history. The consequences of claiming benefits early can have a major financial impact on you and your spouse's well-being for the average household.

Social Security benefits can be claimed at a reduced level at age 62. The full retirement age is dependent upon your birthday as signified by the chart below. If claiming is delayed past full retirement age, there is a delayed retirement credit of 8% per year up to age 70. After age 70, there is no delayed retirement credits. In addition, the spousal benefit does not earn delayed credits past the full retirement age.

Full Retirement Age - Age entitled to the full unreduced benefit.

Born 1943-1954 age 66

Born 1955 age 66 and 2 months

Born 1956 age 66 and 4 months

Born 1957 age 66 and 6 months

Born 1958 age 66 and 8 months

Born 1959 age 66 and 10 months

Born 1960 age 67

Between age 62 and your full retirement age, the earnings test will apply for those with earned income. If you retire prior to full retirement age, $1 of benefit will be withheld for every $2 you earn above the limit for that year. During the year you reach full retirement age, your benefits are reduced $1 for every $3 you earn above a higher limit. After you reach full retirement age, you have unlimited earning potential without a reduction in your benefit. Retiring too soon not only can reduce your benefit for life, but you may be penalized under the earnings test for making too much money. This must be taken in consideration before initializing social security benefits.

Social security benefits can be tax free as long as your modified adjusted gross income is below $32,000 for a married couple and $25,000 for a single person. Modified adjusted gross income (MAGI) includes earned and unearned income such as rents, royalties, capital gains, dividends, taxable bond interest, tax free bond interest, interest from certificate of deposit and money market. The only investments excluded from the MAGI rule is distributions from a Roth IRA, Roth 401(k), Roth 403(b) and non-taxable distributions from cash value life insurance. If your MAGI is between $32,000 and less than $44,000 for a married couple and $25,000 but less than $34,000 for a single person, 50% of your social security benefits are subject to taxes. In addition, if your MAGI is above $44,000 for a married couple and $34,000 for a single person, 85% of your social security benefits are subject to ordinary income taxes. By allocating your retirement investments with the right mixture of retirement assets, you can accomplish a tax free retirement.

Utilizing social security claiming strategies to maximize your social security benefits can enhance your tax favored retirement. Due to social security benefits, either having a zero tax bracket or partially taxed, the greater your benefit the more tax favored income you will receive. Therefore, maximizing your social security income through claiming strategies is prudent not only for the tax favored benefit but for other factors such as an inflation adjusted retirement income. This strategy protects you from running out of money during retirement and eliminates stock and bond market risks.

Before we discuss claiming strategies, we must address why so many Americans are taking social security benefits early at age 62, thus reducing their lifetime versus full retirement age benefit.

Many Americans fear the social security administration will run out of money due to the massive number of Baby Boomers entering retirement. The Social Security system has become the largest source of income for most elderly Americans today. When the system was created, it was designed to supplement other sources of income such as pensions, retirement accounts, investments and savings. It was never intended to be the main source of retirement income. According to the Social Security Administration, the Social Security Trust fund is expected to pay out only 79 cents for each dollar of scheduled benefits by 2034 (based on the July 2015 trust fund report). Many Americans fear that social security will not be in existence at their retirement or the benefit will be greatly reduced. In the future, the benefit may be reduced but not go away. Sure, the benefit may be modified and adjusted over the next few years.

However, it will be political suicide for those politicians that allow the system to go defunct. When Alan Greenspan was Federal Reserve chairman, he made the comment that "he could fix social security in 10 minutes and that's with a 5 minute coffee break." Many analysts agree that social security is the easiest of our federal government's major problems to fix. The biggest ticket item that causes our deficits to swell to unmanageable levels is health care. It is up to the politicians to tackle the funding problem of our country's most sacred program, social security.

Unfortunately, there seems to be little will in Washington to do so due to upsetting too many voters. However, as this issue of threatening reductions in benefit becomes a crisis in a few years, politicians will no longer be able to procrastinate in fixing the problem. The "tin can" will no longer be "kicked down the road" until a future date. When it becomes a crisis, I believe the problem will be addressed.

Social Security Claiming Strategies

By waiting until your full retirement age or until age 70, you will receive a higher tax advantaged income payout. For every dollar increase in benefit, assuming your MAGI is below the Social Security taxation threshold, all of your income is tax free.

However, even if your MAGI goes above the first threshold, only 50% of your benefit is subject to income taxes. This means fifty percent of your income is tax free. In addition, if you go above the second threshold, 15% of your benefit is tax free and only 85% is subject to income taxes. Due to only a portion of the income being subject to income taxes in the higher thresholds, the income source is very tax advantaged. That's why you need to maximize your social security retirement income benefit. There are only a few investments that give you tax advantaged income, a guaranteed lifetime income stream and inflation protection.

By waiting until age 70, a delayed retirement credit of 8% per year will increase your social security income. If your full retirement age is 66, a 32% increase in your benefit can be realized. If inflation increases by 3% per year, you will have an 11% increase per year with a 44% increase in benefit. With longer life expectancies, this strategy can be very beneficial to either your spouse or yourself while living. Since women have longer life expectancies than men, claiming your benefit at age 70 can greatly benefit your wife especially if she is a few years younger than you.

For individuals retiring prior to age 70, consider spending down other retirement assets to bridge the "gap period" to maximize your benefit. Let's assume you retire at age 66 and want to maximize your benefit by waiting to claim the benefit at age 70 or you are age

62 and want to maximize your benefit by waiting until your full retirement age. By spending down retirement assets during the gap period can allow your social security benefits to grow. The best asset to use for spend down will depend upon your financial situation. However, sometimes IRA assets should be considered for individuals who potentially may see their social security benefits taxed or taxed at higher levels due to required minimum distributions at age 70 ½. For those preparing for retirement, you should consider creating a social security spend down fund to bridge the gap between your retirement date and either your full retirement age or the maximum social security claiming age of 70.

Social security claiming strategies warrant a discussion on breakeven analysis for social security benefits. Breakeven analysis helps you determine financially at what age you will receive the maximum payout given the hypothetical situation being constructed. The key component of this analysis is longevity which is so variable based on the individual. In this example, I'm assuming a full retirement benefit at age 66 of $2,000 per month with an annual inflation adjustment of 3% with a life expectancy to age 95. Compare claiming at age 66 versus age 62, your breakeven point is age 76.

Therefore, if you live past age 76, you will be better off financially to have waited until age 66 to claim benefits. Comparing age 70 to age 62, your breakeven point is age 79. Comparing age 70 to age 66, your breakeven point is age 81. Even if you don't live to age 90 or to 100, it makes financial sense to delay your benefit. In addition, claiming Social Security at age 62, assuming a $1,500 per month payment, the total benefit at age 95 is $1,039,143.

Claiming the Social Security benefit at age 66, assuming a $2,000 per month payment, the total benefit at age 95 is $1,285,117. Lastly, claiming Social Security at age 70, assuming a payment of $2,640 per month, the total benefit at age 95 is $1,531,112. For those individuals or couples that anticipate on living longer, delaying the benefit as long as possible makes financial sense. Living beyond the "breakeven points," increases your lifetime retirement benefits. The "restricted application" claiming strategy is designed for couples who both have an earnings history that may retire at different ages. This is how it works: an individual at full retirement age can collect benefits from their spouse while allowing their benefit to earn delayed retirement credits.

For example, let's assume husband and wife want to retire at the same time at ages 66 and 62. They both will earn $2,000 per month at their full retirement age. Because the wife has not reached the full retirement age, her benefit will be reduced. However, if she files for the benefit at age 62 earning $1,500 per month while her husband files a "restricted application" and chooses a spousal benefit of $1,000 per month then switches to his benefit at age 70 with $2,640 per month, they will potentially have more lifetime income. If they had both taken their benefit without filing a restricted application, their total monthly income is $3,500 versus $2,500 per month with a restricted application. At age 70, the couple's benefit will increase due to the delayed retirement credits to $4,140 ($1,500 + $2,640 = $4,140). The annual income difference is $7,680 per year by waiting 4 years.

The breakeven point for utilizing this strategy is 6 years assuming no inflation adjustments. In addition, you should consider creating a fund to bridge the gap until you receive the maximum retirement benefit. This will give you a greater and more secure retirement for the future. With changes under the Bipartisan Budget Act of 2015, "restricted application" is only available to individuals who were 62 prior to 1/1/2016.

One of the biggest mistakes business owners make every year is taking S-Corporation distributions versus W-2 income to avoid paying social security and Medicare taxes. The theory of thought is that if you do not pay taxes, you will have more money to invest for retirement. Unfortunately, few people ever save the money. It typically goes toward lifestyle spending. As the business owner enters into retirement, he has little money and a modest social security income to live on for the remainder of his life. In addition, if the spouse is working in the family business, no salary is paid and no social security benefit created, compounding their retirement income problem. However, the unpaid spouse will have access to the spousal and survivor benefits. Because social security income is so tax advantaged and increases with inflation, maximizing these benefits is a very important part of a secure retirement plan. If you are in this situation, you should consider discussing this issue with your CPA.

A major hardship on couples is losing social security income when a spouse dies during retirement. The social security administration allows the higher of the two social security benefits to be given to the surviving spouse. For example, a homemaker may receive one half of her husband's social security benefits while both are living. At death, she will receive her husband's higher benefit while losing hers. The retirement budget often depends on both social security incomes to maintain the living spouse's basic household expenses. For most, the surviving spouse's household budget doesn't decrease substantially. Generally, the surviving spouse will need 70% to 100% of the couple's' income.

Underestimating your spouse's income needs during retirement can be devastating. Making decisions on purchasing your prescription medication versus buying groceries is not an appropriate position to be in during retirement. This predicament causes the surviving spouse to liquidate retirement assets until it's all gone. Making certain both income streams are still available after a spouse's death is critical. A tax advantaged strategy for replacing social security benefits of a deceased spouse is to purchase life insurance and invest the death proceeds into an immediate annuity. The death benefit will be paid to the surviving spouse tax free and the immediate annuity will provide a tax favored monthly income guaranteed for life.

Economic Lifestyle of a
Married Couple

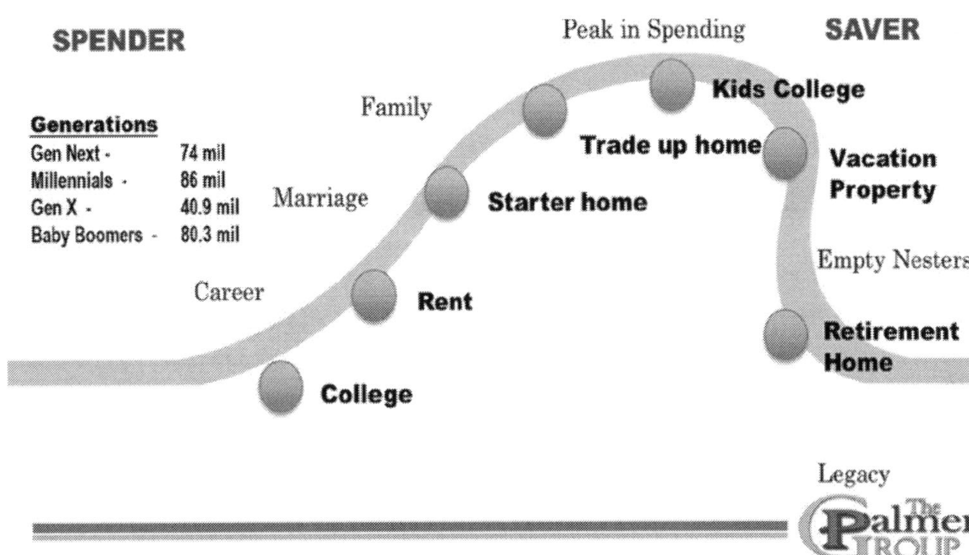

Why Taxes May Increase in the Future

"In 1790, the nation which had fought a revolution against taxation without representation discovered that some of its citizens weren't much happier about taxation with representation."

~Lyndon B. Johnson

There's a good chance income tax rates will increase and deductions will decrease or be eliminated in the future due to the need for tax revenue by Federal, State and Municipal Governments. The purpose of this chapter is not political. It's an observation based on demographics of the US population and what may happen in the future. To explain how demographics make a significant impact on the economy, let's review the life cycle of a typical American household. The Baby Boom generation (born from 1946 to 1964) is the largest population group to ever go through an American economy. They've made ripple effects in the economy as they have progressed through their life stages. Ken Dychtwald, Gerontologist, states it best "the baby boomers are like a pig going through the digestive tract of a python." As the snake digests the pig, the snake expands to accommodate the size of the pig. The US economy has been in an expansion phase for many years due to the spending patterns of the Baby Boomers. However, there is a contraction period as this group enters into retirement. To understand the past and project the future, our spending patterns through our life stages must be examined.

When you graduate high school, you either enter into the workforce or pursue a higher education. When you enter into the workforce, you became a participant in the economy by renting an apartment or house and purchasing items such as furnishings, clothing, technology, and vehicles. When the baby boomers entered into this life stage, they caused inflation because there was too much money running after too few goods and services. Several of you can remember when finance rates were 15% on mortgages and certificates of deposits were paying high interest rates. It was the best of times and the worst of times for the economy.

After marriage, the Baby Boomers progressed from the rental stage to becoming first time home buyers. Up fitting the house with life's necessities expands the economy especially when there are 80.3 million people doing it over a short period of time. As the household formation period expands with children, the starter home becomes a tight fit. They upgrade from the starter home to the trade up home further stimulating the economy. When my second child arrived on the scene, toys and stuff were everywhere in our small home. So, we decided to trade up into a much bigger house to accommodate our lifestyle needs. As millions of Americans traded up, real estate values began to increase steadily. The building industry saw one of the largest expansions in US history enabling steady growth in the economy. In turn it brought in a significant amount of tax revenue for the federal, state and municipal governments. Jobs were easy to find and who ever wanted to work had employment.

The American household, including the Baby Boomers, then reach peak spending when their kids go to college. Most families during this stage are spending more than they bring in during this period due to paying for college expenses and maintaining their household expenses. In essence, we are essentially maintaining multiple households at the same time. During this stage of life, there is little money for saving and investing due to trying to launch our kids into this world.

After we have launched our kids into their careers, the more affluent often seek to purchase second homes in places they may want to relocate during retirement. Popular areas for retirement are warmer climates with beaches or mountains. As we have more discretionary household income, the retirement reality hits us square in the eyes. "I'm only a few years away from retirement and I don't have enough money saved." We move from the spending cycle of our life to the saving cycle of our life. In preparation for retirement, we begin to reduce debt, increase retirement contributions and seek advice on how to create a nest egg large enough to meet our retirement income needs.

As the Baby Boomers enter retirement, many of them will downsize their personal residences. This often happens when they come to the realization that the grandkids are not coming to visit as they initially thought. Also, they are no longer interested in the cleaning and maintenance that a house requires. It's easier to downsize into a property that meets their current needs often to a one level home, town house or condo. Many will use the proceeds from the sale of their house to supplement retirement or payoff outstanding debt to improve their retirement lifestyle. They apply for social security benefits between age 62 and age 70 depending on their retirement date. At age 65, they will be eligible for Medicare.

As millions of baby boomers retire, this will put major stress on entitlement programs increasing federal deficits potentially forcing politicians to make difficult cuts in entitlement programs and/or increase taxes to maintain the programs.

Since the baby boom generation has been the largest population group to go through the American economy, they have expanded the economy throughout their lifecycle. It will be no different as they enter into the retirement years. The increased need for tax revenue will be evident to pay for government benefits such as social security and Medicare.

The social security administration publishes on its website that the benefits may not be there in the future and that if the plan is not modified, the benefits will be reduced. Whether there are tax increases or reduced benefits (which function like a tax increase), you and I will pay the bill. Medicare has the potential, according to pundits, to potentially bankrupt the United States by itself. I don't know whether this is true or not, but logical sense is that 80.3 million baby boomers aging and needing health care will provide a massive challenge to taxpayers. Going back to my earlier analogy, the pig has made it to the end of the digestive tract of the python and has no other place to go. As there is expansion in the need for health care, travel and entertainment, there is contraction in other parts of the economy and Generation X is not large enough to keep the economic engine going at the same pace as the Baby Boomers.

Generation X which is 40.9 million in population is insufficient to pay for the 80.3 million baby boomers' entitlement programs. Gen X is one half the size of the Baby Boomers which will put a strain on economic expansion. Contraction in the economy is more probable due to the limited size of this population group and therefore less tax revenue unless increases are realized through loss of deductions and marginal tax rate increases.

Since 2008, the Federal Reserve has worked overtime trying to stimulate our economy and put people back to work after the real estate crash and bank failures. We have experienced contraction in the economy making our government utilize unproven tactics to stimulate the economy such as quantitative easing by the Federal Reserve. Since that time, taxes have increased on almost all Americans through payroll taxes, loss of deductions and marginal tax rate increases for the highest taxpayers. This trend may continue over the next several years as mounting pressures occur due to increased health care needs with millions of baby boomers entering retirement, draining the Social Security system.

The Millennial generation is larger than the baby boom generation. This population group over the next few years will be entering into the household formation stage of their life. However, this generation has racked up a tremendous amount of school debt that may lessen their impact in the economy in the short run.

Also, many in this population group have experienced difficulty in finding jobs which has forced them to move back in with parents. If history repeats itself, when the baby boomers entered the household formation stage, there was inflation due to the mere size of the group buying starter homes and starting families. Remember that inflation is too much money chasing too few goods and services. As the Millennia's enter this life stage, higher inflation could be an issue again.

Furthermore, as the economy has transformed into a World economy over the last two decades, analysts have pointed out there may be a billion people in the emerging markets moving from poverty into the middle class over the next few years creating a vast demand for consumer products. We may be competing with the rest of the world for goods and services causing price increases. By having some inflation, the national debt is decreased and it's easier to pay back the monies we have borrowed. However, massive inflation can cause major problems to our economy. It will be up to the Federal Reserve board and politicians to navigate us through this mine field.

The next several years are going to be quite interesting as these dynamics play out in the United States and World economies. The population trends in the US seem to suggest the potential for higher taxes, some inflation and the potential for government spending cuts. If we have higher taxes in the future, the tax free bucket will be your best

Rally in keeping your taxes low and for you to be able to maintain your lifestyle. The key is to hedge your retirement portfolio against higher taxes in the future by being tax diversified.

How High Can Tax Rates GO?

Politically it's popular in the United States to go after the guys who have all of the money. So, the most productive citizens in our society pay a larger portion of the tax burden. Whether you think this is fair or unfair, the reality is that the more money you make, the more taxes you pay. This philosophy emerged soon after the United States created the tax code in 1913.

The following chart shows the lowest marginal income tax rate and the highest marginal income tax rate on the wealthy by decade. For example, between 1990 and 1999, the top taxpayers paid 28% until politicians voted to increase the income tax rate to 39.6%. So the lowest top marginal tax rate for the wealthy in that decade was 28% and the highest top marginal tax rate was 39.6%.

Tax Rates on the Wealthy

Decade Rate	Lowest top Marginal Tax Rate	Highest top Marginal -Tax Rate
2010-present	35%	39.6%
2000-2009	35%	39.6%
1990-1999	28%	39.6%
1980-1989	28%	70%
1970-1979	70%	70%
1960-1969	70%	91%
1950-1959	91%	92%
1940-1949	79%	94%
1930-1939	25%	79%
1920-1929	25%	73%
1913-1919	7%	77%

SOURCE: Tax Foundation, Federal Individual Income Tax History Nominal Dollars, Income Years 1913-2013

As you see in this chart, the wealthy are in one of the lowest top marginal income tax rates in history. The highest marginal income tax rates came in the 1940's topping off at 94% of income. It's been a political argument since the tax code was established if higher or lower tax rates is the best solution to fund government spending. Everyone seems to have a strong political opinion surrounding this subject. Whether you are Democrat, Republican or Independent, it seems that the majority of people in all economic classes do not want to pay more than their fair share of the tax burden.

The big question is, "Will history repeat itself?" Will tax rates continue to rise as the Federal government tries to take care of its elderly population issue as the Baby Boomers are fully in retirement? Politics will play an important role in answering this question as the government deals with its fiscal issues. However, the ingredients are in place for the potential of higher taxes in the future. Prudent financial planning is necessary as you take this into account when developing your retirement plan.

Source: US Census Projections for 2013 based on 2010 census. Peter Francese, US Census. Barron's' article– On the Rise, 4/29/2013.

Protecting the Three Buckets °

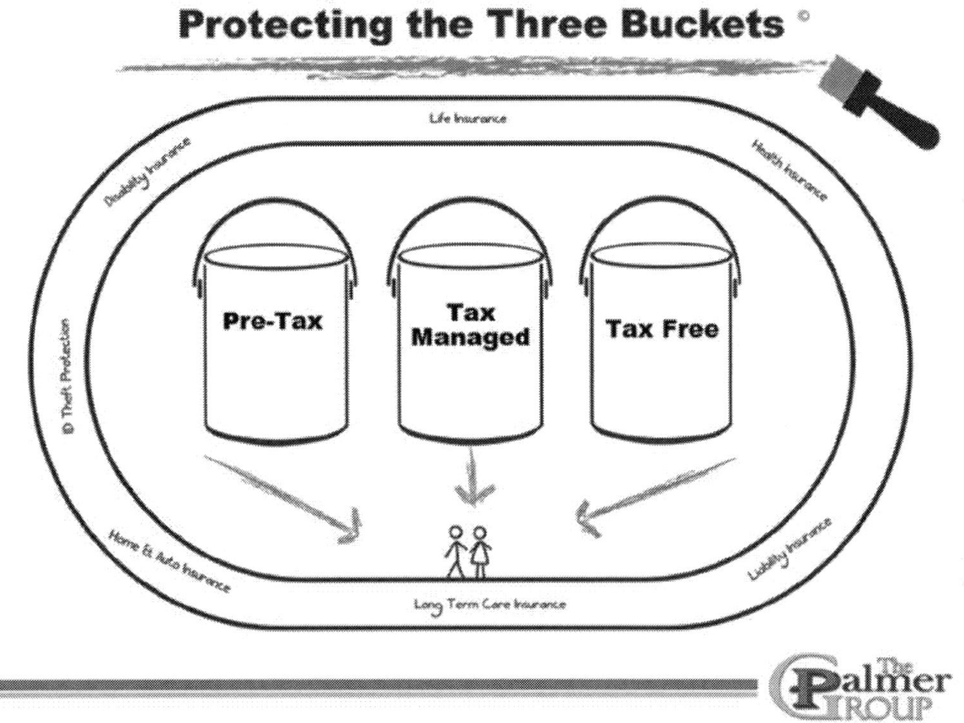

Chapter 7

Protecting the Three Tax Buckets

"I am proud to be paying taxes in the United States. The only thing is I could be just as proud for half of the money."

~Arthur Godfrey

It would be remiss to discuss creating wealth in the most efficient way possible without discussing how to protect the wealth you are trying to create or maintain. We spend most of our life accumulating wealth to try to do basically three things. First, we save money to meet family emergencies and short- term needs. Second, we save and invest to give our children a "leg up" on life through a good college education. Third, we save to take care of ourselves during retirement to enjoy the fruits of our labor. Retirement is supposed to be a time of fun and relaxation, reconnecting with friends and family, travel and hobbies. We have worked our entire life to get to the promised land of retirement. It would be devastating if this was taken away from you due to risks you are accepting with your money. So, let's take a look at how to protect the three buckets of money during the accumulation stage as well as the income stage of retirement.

As we build these buckets of money over our lifetime, there are things that can happen and go wrong that can financially devastate our buckets. In order to protect the buckets, we must make sure there is adequate insurance protection in place to protect the buckets.

I'm going to go through risk management and give you a few true stories of how managing these risks have paid off handsomely.

Health Insurance

Health insurance is a risk management tool that can keep a family from going bankrupt. For example, my daughter was born with a birth defect called spina bifida. Spina bifida, causes many health issues. She's had 24 surgeries and multiple hospitalizations. Our health insurance has paid out over $2,000,000 tax free (to me) to the providers that have saved her life. If I had not insured this risk, my buckets of money would have been completely devastated. Yes, I do pay health insurance premiums, but it's been worth it. It has allowed me to stay on track for retirement and save for my children's college education without them having to borrow the funds for their education.

Life Insurance

A few years ago, an acquaintance from church died from a heart attack while playing a softball game in the church softball league. He was in his 40's with two children and one child with special needs. To complicate matters, his wife didn't work outside the home due to the special needs child requiring special attention. It was very shocking to our church community that he died so young. However, the real shock was watching the aftermath of his desperate wife dealing with financial issues. See, he had limited life insurance and financial resources to provide for his wife and kids. A few days after his funeral, his wife's college ex-boyfriend shows up on the scene vowing that he would take care of her if she would marry him. He was recently divorced and still had feelings for his former girlfriend. She accepted the offer and they were married one month from the date of her husband's death. Did she marry out of love or desperation? My vote is desperation! The marriage lasted a couple of years and ended in divorce. If he had owned enough life insurance to protect his family, I wonder if things would have turned out differently. Owning the appropriate amount of life insurance not only fills the buckets with cash the family needs, but it is a love gift left behind letting them know you cared. I personally want my wife and children to maintain their lifestyle and not have to worry about money. Not having to worry about money is truly a wonderful final love gift to the most cherished people in your life.

Disability Insurance

One of your greatest risks to filling up the buckets of money is the loss of your "human capital." You may be wondering, "What is human capital?" Human capital is your ability to get up out of bed every morning and go to work. It is the sum total of your lifetime earnings. When you are in your 20's and 30's, you have a tremendous amount of human capital due to the number of years left before retirement. As you age, human capital becomes less and less each year making you dependent upon your investments during retirement. Human capital can be shortened by a disability caused by a sickness or accident. Also, it can be lengthened by working longer. Let's assume you are 25 years old and have 40 years left in your working career. You currently are earning $50,000 per year with a potential 5% increase in earnings every year until age 65. Your human capital is worth an estimated $6,000,000. If you have an accident or illness that causes a lifelong disability, $6 million dollars is a lot of money to forfeit. In addition, the three buckets will never be filled with assets for your future. You will lose your independence and be left depending on government, family and friends for assistance.

The chances of you becoming disabled is your highest potential risk between now and retirement. But, few people purchase disability insurance to protect themselves. Most people don't have enough money for short-term emergencies versus having enough cash resources to manage a disability that may last a lifetime. Bankruptcy and poverty may be your future if this risk isn't eliminated.

Long-term Care Insurance

There is a myth that young people don't have long- term care events. There are numerous instances where young people are plagued with an illness or accidents that leave them needing assistance for their lifetime. A long-term care event is defined as being unable to perform two of six activities of daily living (ADL's) comprised of eating, bathing, toileting, transferring, incontinence, dressing or a cognitive impairment. My wife worked at a rehab hospital with head injured patients as a speech pathologist. Most of the victims were young males taking recreational or occupational risks. Most would qualify under the definitions of long-term care due to the loss of 2 of the 6 ADLs or the cognitive impairment. You don't have to be old to have a need for long-term care insurance. My wife and I personally purchased our long-term care insurance in our early 40's to protect our assets and our sanity if either one of us had a long-term care event. We've been care taking for a disabled child for the last 18 years with no assistance. I can't imagine care taking of a spouse as we are raising our family and growing our business.

The aging process can bring on devastating risks to our retirement income due to failing health or an accident that causes a long-term care event. The cost for a long-term care event can be staggering to a family's financial resources. That's the reason why having long-term care insurance is vitally important to protect your buckets of money. Most long-term care is provided at home by unpaid caregivers such as a spouse or family member. I've seen situations where adult children had no other choice but to quit their jobs to take care of an aging parent. This hardship often causes marital and financial stress upon their children.

I had a client whose wife had Alzheimer's disease. He told me, in order to mow his yard, he would gently and loosely tie a rope around his wife's waist and have her follow him as he pushed the lawn mower. Someone had to monitor her 24 hours per day to maintain her safety. I witnessed a healthy spouse caregiver die before her aging husband due to the relentless day after day stress of taking care of her husband. I've seen a son put his mom in an Alzheimer's unit draining all of her financial fortune that could have benefited multiple generations in her family. My dad had to sell our family farm to take care of my grandfather's long-term care event due to being a double amputee from diabetes. The hundreds of acres of farm land would be worth millions today enabling my sister and me a greater sense of financial security.

In my opinion, one of the greatest gifts that you can give your children is to purchase long-term care insurance or a life insurance policy with a long-term care rider for your care. They will thank you greatly for this gift when the day comes that you will need to use it. You can't ignore the odds of having a long-term care event and the potential devastation it may have on your family's finances, emotional and physical health. The chances of a female, age 65, needing long-term care before she dies is 79% and a male has a 58% chance of having a long- term care event before he dies.* The odds are too great to ignore or to try to self-insure this risk.

Identity Theft

Identity theft is becoming a prominent industry for thieves. Corporations spend millions of dollars each year trying to protect your financial information.

When identity theft occurs, it can take hours of time and money to clear your good name or potentially recapture the assets that were stolen. Having identity theft protection can help prevent or help clear your name if this thievery happens to you.

Property & Casualty

Maintaining adequate homeowners insurance is often required by mortgage companies in case of fire or theft. Homes appreciate in value over time and building costs increase over time. Have your property and casualty agent give you potential replacement costs on your home and insure it fully. Over the last 25 years, I've had clients lose their home and business due to fire. When asked, "What was the most difficult issue in recapturing the loss," they stated that the structure itself was the easiest to obtain reimbursement for. The difficult issue was trying to remember all of the contents and proving the condition of the contents prior to the fire for reimbursement. It is wise to take photos or videos of your possessions and store them in an area that can be easily accessed if a fire destroys your home or business.

Umbrella Coverage

Consider maintaining adequate umbrella coverage that protects your home and autos in the event of a lawsuit. A serious car accident that disables or kills someone due to an accident that is deemed your fault can bankrupt a person. Typical coverage ranges are from $1,000,000 up to $5,000,000. It's important as we build our wealth through tax strategies and wise invests that protect the three buckets of money in the event something does go wrong. It's not a matter of will something go wrong; it is a matter of when. You need to be protected or you could lose a lifetime of hard work.

*American Association of Long-term care insurance. The source book for long-term care information, 2006 Edition, 2005 US Census Bureau data.

Three Layers of Diversification

Chapter 8

The Three Layers of Diversification

"Divide your portion to seven, or even to eight, for you do not know what misfortune may occur on the earth."

~ Ecclesiastes 11:2

We have all heard the saying, "don't put all of your eggs in one basket." This is very true when investing for retirement. Proper diversification is allocating your investment capital among diverse and uncorrelated asset classes. Asset allocation is the cornerstone of diversification whether your assets are in large company stocks, small company stocks, foreign stocks, bonds, commodities, real estate, etc. As we approach retirement, asset allocation has a more limited role compared to a more suitable product allocation. You and your financial advisor will have to make a decision on how much of your retirement income will come from conventional investments such as mutual funds, exchange traded funds, stocks and bonds versus pension like products such as immediate annuities, variable annuities with lifetime income guarantees and other guaranteed life insurance products. As you transition from wealth accumulation to income generation, you will be faced with very different risks that didn't exist during the pre-retirement years. The BIG 4 (RISKS).

The Big 4 is what I call the four major risks that retirees face as they move into the income generation stage of retirement planning. Please note that these risks are not inclusive of all risks that retiree's face. I've nicknamed these my Big 4 as being the most probable risks. The Big 4 are longevity risk, inflation risk, taxes and sequence of return risk. Each of these risks can be devastating to a retiree's retirement income. We need to examine each and discuss solutions on how to avoid or minimize these risks.

Longevity Risk

There is good news and bad news about getting old! The good news is that we are living longer due to medical technology and healthier living. The bad news is that living for long periods of time requires a significant nest egg for retirement.

According to the US Annuity 2000 mortality tables by the Society of Actuaries, the expected life span of individuals and couples age 65 has increased. There is a 50% chance for a couple age 65, that one of them will live to age 92. A 65 year old male has a 50% chance to live to age 85 and a female to age 88.

Furthermore, a 65 year old couple has a 25% chance of one of them living until age 97. There are several factors that play into our longevity such as lifestyle factors, behavioral habits and family history. The critical point here is that the human lifespan is random. We simply don't know how long we will live. Therefore our retirement strategy must account for longevity risk so we don't become bankrupt in our retirement years.

There is a misconception about withdrawal rates from investments at retirement. The conventional wisdom of the past is that you can withdraw 5% from an investment and it will sustain your retirement income for the rest of your life. However, as Kelley Greene points out in a Wall Street Journal article titled "Say Goodbye to the 4% Rule," that with income distributions "2% is bullet proof, 3% is probably safe, 4% is pushing it, and, at 5% you're eating Alpo in your old age."

Sustainable withdrawal rates are much less than most people think during the retirement years. Taking too much income, with the wrong sequence of returns during the income stage, will cause you to run out of money.

Taxes

Since I've dedicated most of this book to discussing taxes, I will only reiterate that due to demographics, deficits and government spending, there's a good chance tax rates will increase in the future. Your retirement income may be squeezed significantly if you don't appropriately allocate assets in the right tax buckets. Tax strategy will be a key component in your quest to not outlive your money during the income years.

Inflation Risk

If you are like me, inflation is gauged at the gas pump and the grocery store. My family drinks a lot of milk. Over the years, I've noticed that the price per gallon has increased on a consistent basis.

This is what you call inflation. Inflation is the cost of goods and services going up on a year by year basis. The Consumer Price Index (CPI) is one of the measures of inflation which the U.S. Federal Reserve monitors. For retirees, there is a consumer price index for the elderly (CPI-E) that monitors the spending habits of retirees. Retirees tend to spend money a little differently than a 30 year old. For example, inflation as monitored by the CPI since 1982 is at 2.9%, but inflation for the elderly (CPI-E) has paced at a 3.1% rate. Even with modest inflation, this can take a toll on a retiree's income over a 20 year period of time. For example, if your income during retirement was $4,000 per month in today's dollars with a 3.1% inflation rate for 20 years, your buying power will erode to $2,131.

Stated another way, you will need $7,366 per month to buy the same goods and services that $4,000 per month buys today. If your retirement income plan doesn't take inflation into account during your distribution years, you most likely will be forced to liquidate your principal or cut back drastically on your lifestyle to fund your retirement needs. You will be in the danger zone of running out of money during retirement.

Health care inflation is even worse with an average increase of 5.1% since 1982 and a 13% increase since 2008. With changes in health care laws and as baby boomers start to retire, this trend is unlikely to change.

The average couple will spend $220,000 in medical expenses excluding long-term care. Furthermore, a couple will have a 70% chance that one of them will have a long-term care event with in-home care costing an estimated $40,000 per year and nursing home care an average of $80,000 per year. That's why you must plan for a sizable health care budget within your retirement income plan.

Sequence of Return Risk

Most investors have never heard of sequence of return risk. The reason is, for those in the accumulation stage of their life, this risk doesn't exist. You simply average out your returns over the accumulation stage and it doesn't matter what sequence they come in. However, when you enter the income distribution period of your life, sequence of returns will determine if your retirement years are golden or if you are a resident at the local homeless shelter. If you receive negative returns on your investments early in retirement, the sustainability of your spending will be greatly diminished.

Unfortunately, no one, not even your investment advisor, can protect you from negative returns in an inevitable bear market. No one has control over the timing, length and size of the correction. Furthermore, no one has control over inflation, when looking at the length and cost of your retirement until your death.

To emphasize the importance to mitigate the sequence of return risk in your portfolio, let's assume you have a $1,000,000 stock portfolio entering the retirement income years.

Unfortunately, your timing is imperfect with a 2008 like correction as you begin withdrawing $50,000 per year (5%) from your investment portfolio. From the top of the market to the bottom, you have a 50% decline in portfolio value. With no distributions from the portfolio, $1,000,000 has been reduced to $500,000 due to the 50% correction.

It will take a 100% rate of return to wipe out a 50% loss. If you are taking a $50,000 distribution in year one of retirement, you will need to earn a 122% rate of return to get you back to your initial value. Devastating losses during the early distribution years will either force you back into the workforce or minimize your retirement.

With a product allocation strategy, you don't have to predict the outcomes of random events. You basically insure against adverse outcomes guaranteeing your investment income streams during retirement. There are three basic income strategies to be considered in a comprehensive product allocation strategy.

First, is the systematic withdrawal plan in which you systematically withdraw funds from a diversified portfolio to generate a retirement income. The systematic withdrawal plan may help with inflation risk, liquidity risk and may potentially leave a sizable estate to heirs. This will be dependent solely on the sequence of returns of the investments. With this process, the systematic withdrawal is repeated until you consume the entire account value or when you die. There are no guarantees in income stream with this strategy.

Second, are variable and indexed annuities that have guaranteed lifetime income riders ensuring against sequence of return risk, longevity risk and other risks associated with retirement.

Third, is the lifetime payout income annuity (immediate annuities) which promises to pay a steady, fixed payment as long as you live. This structure is very similar to disappearing traditional pension plans that mitigate longevity risk and behavioral risk. Behavioral risk is best described when an investor buys stocks when there's euphoria in the markets and sells when fear is exacerbated in the markets. In essence you are buying high and selling low which is totally opposite of how an investor should react. In order to have a sustainable retirement, a mixture of all three of these methods may be necessary.

Obtaining the right mixture is key to a successful retirement. You will want to make sure your retirement nest egg is diversified across multiple asset classes versus specific economic sectors or industries. Product diversification will become significantly more important during the distribution stage. In addition, you will want to obtain help from a competent advisor that will help you diversify your retirement portfolio from a tax, product and asset allocation perspective. These are the key ingredients in baking a beautiful and delicious retirement cake.

* Source: March 2, 2012, Consumer Price Index for the Elderly, TED: The Economics Daily. www.bls.gov/opub/ted/2012/ted_20120302.htm.

** Source: Prudential Research Report, Long-term Care Cost Study, 2010
*** Source: Fidelity Investments retiree health costs estimate. 2013. Health care and nursing home costs may vary by state.
**** Source: National Clearinghouse for long-term care information, US Department of Health and Human Services
***** Source: Prudential. Four Pillars of Retirement Series, Planning for Retirement: The distribution of Lifetime Health care costs.

Chapter 9

Retirement Income Pyramid

"In the end, it's not the years in your life that count.

It's the life in your years."

~Abraham Lincoln

Retirement Income Pyramid

Wants
- Stocks
- Bonds
- Alternatives

Needs
- Social Security
- Pension
- Annuities

Legacy
- Stocks
- Bonds
- Alternatives
- Life Insurance

Emergencies
- Cash/Cash Equivalents
- Bonds

The Palmer Group

Retirement Income Pyramid

Wants
(Discretionary Spending)
- Travel
- Hobbies
- Entertainment
- Spoil Grandchildren

Needs
(Basic Expenses)
- Housing
- Food
- Insurance
- Health Care
- Transportation

Legacy
- Special Needs
- Education
- Family Well Being
- Charity
- Multigenerational Wealth

Emergencies
- Health Issues
- Stock/Bond Market
  Corrections
- Family Needs
- Other

Whether you are 30 years old or 65 years old, knowing your budget is extremely important. Budgets are typically broken down into absolute necessities (Needs) such as housing, transportation, insurance, food, and health care. Discretionary spending (Wants) include things like travel, hobbies, entertainment, and economic outpatient support to kids and grandkids. Having a projected retirement budget is very important to determine the amount of wealth needed to provide the required income streams to support yourself in retirement. If you have too much budget and not enough income, you will need to reconsider your retirement date. If you are bull headed and retire anyway, life is going to get really tough! I can give you multiple cases where people didn't listen to advice and retired anyway and are suffering the consequences of their decision. In several cases, they failed to factor in inflation, higher taxes, sequence of return risk and longevity risk. A few are on a collision course running out of money and some have returned to work to rebuild their financial resources. Projected retirement budgets should be projected as early as in your twenties to put you on the "glide path" to financial independence.

Maintaining appropriate emergency cash is essential in managing risks in retirement. Risks to retirement cash flow can be everything from a major repair with your home, replacing a vehicle, health issue, family emergency and/or a financial market correction. The typical emergency fund during your accumulation years is 4 to 6 months of living expenses. The appropriate emergency fund going into retirement should represent 12 to 36 months of living expenses. You may wonder why

so much money in emergency reserves during retirement? The Perfect Storm could happen where the financial markets are in free fall and you are in need of significant cash from your investments to meet a specific need. Having a large emergency fund will allow you to turn off the stock income spigot in order to wait for a recovery in your non- guaranteed income streams. Selling stocks at depressed levels to provide for income is a recipe for disaster especially early in your retirement.

When the market recovers, you cease tapping your emergency fund turning on the stock income streams once again. The main purpose of the emergency fund from this day forward is to protect your retirement income. If you spend down retirement generating assets for emergencies, you will eventually run out of money during retirement. Think of the emergency fund as a Marvel Action Hero (such as Super Man or Spider Man) coming to the rescue when chaos breaks loose.

For many, legacy planning is very important at all economic and net worth levels. It's important to help out future generations because our kids and grandkids may not have the same opportunity in the future as we've had in the past. Leaving financial resources to better their lives is a prevailing and honorable goal whether it's setting aside funds while living or creating funds at death for educational purposes, creating businesses or just helping heirs get ahead in life. Also, special needs families worry about who is going to provide care for their loved ones if they are unable to do so. Leaving funds in special needs trusts, to protect their government sponsored benefits, is important to maintain their quality of life. Lastly, many have philanthropic wishes to provide for the greater good of society. Giving to charity while living and at death can be a noble cause.

Since the retirement budget is broken down into "Needs and Wants," how assets are invested for each component is very important. The "Needs" which represent your life sustaining necessities should contain guaranteed lifetime income streams. Income streams that meet these criteria are such things as Social Security Benefits, Pension income, and guaranteed income annuities. The "Needs" portion of your budget is the most important part of your budget and must be protected. If this part of your income is eliminated through a spend down of assets due to unforeseen circumstances, you don't get a second chance. That's why guaranteed income streams are so important.

The 'Wants' portion of the budget is the most flexible portion of the budget. I've had people tell me that this portion is as important as the 'Needs' portion. In any case, if financial markets go down, you can always pull back on your spending in this category. Having assets positioned in traditional investments such as mutual funds, exchange traded funds, stocks, bonds and alternatives is appropriate. You will need to make the choice to have non-guaranteed or guaranteed income streams to satisfy this portion of the budget.

The emergency fund must be very liquid with very little investment risk. These funds need to be invested in cash or cash equivalents. Low risk bond mutual funds may be appropriate as well. These funds do not need to be correlated with the stock market. Often, emergency cash is needed when there has been a "blood bath" on Wall Street.

The legacy assets are assets not needed for income and emergency purposes. These assets may be invested for 20 to 30 years with no income distributions. The assets should be invested for growth and you can afford to take more investment risk with the assets. The assets can be invested in stocks, bonds and alternatives. To leverage these assets, life insurance can be purchased providing a tax free guaranteed death benefit to enhance the cash pile for heirs or charities.

Chapter 10

Financial Planning, Indispensable

"In preparing for battle, I have always found that plans are useless, but planning is indispensable."

~ Dwight D. Eisenhower

(Quoted in Six Crises by Nixon, Richard (1962). "Khrushchev." Doubleday).

As General Dwight D. Eisenhower led American troops in World War II, he would spend hours planning for the battle. The planning would make him consider the contingencies if the events of the battle didn't proceed as he originally planned.

Having contingency plans would give him the ability to adapt as the unanticipated events unfolded and provide stability and confidence in the midst of chaos. The battle plan would provide alternatives to goals and objectives allowing the General to assess the resources needed to adapt to the present situation. The Financial Planner's role is to help clients adapt quickly to events in their financial world that may affect their future.

In the traditional financial planning process, the planner will make lots of assumptions about the future as seen in the client's eyes. Assumptions will range from retirement lifestyle, anticipated retirement date, inflation rates, presumed growth rates on investments, estimates on how to value social security income and unanticipated health issues. Unfortunately, the assumptions in a financial plan are rarely accurate. We simply can't presume about the future because we don't know what the future will bring. People change their goals/objectives, unexpected life events happen, unexpected World/National events occur, political issues arise and people make mistakes in investing.

Even though your original financial plan may become worthless, the process of planning is indispensable. That's why periodically meeting with your financial planner is critical to discuss contingencies for the battle when needed. The battle corrections are very important if you plan on winning the War. That's why people need a planner versus a plan. Your long-term financial success is dependent on your willingness to make battle changes.

So, are financial plans worthless? No, they are your most critical action step to build a secure financial future. Unfortunately, people will often throw the baby out with the bath water as soon as turmoil strikes their financial plan. As soon as an uncertain event arises, such as a deterioration in the economy or uncertainty about a tax law, they shelve their financial plan waiting until the conditions improve. Successful people would never consider such a passive response to be acceptable at their work or business.

There are 80.3 million Baby Boomers (born between 1946 and 1964) that have prepared very little for retirement. The Baby Boomers are living through boom and bust times in our economy and financial system. They may become America's longest working generation if they don't get busy saving, investing and reducing debt. This is no time to be a "do it yourselfer". Hire a fee based financial planner to help you navigate through uncharted waters. It's time for you to have laser focus on your retirement goals, time-sensitive accountability for each step necessary to build a secure financial future and benchmarks for their achievement.

Here's How to Cut Your Taxes and Keep More of Your Savings

You already know saving for retirement is a critical step in ensuring a successful retirement lifestyle. The confusing part is not knowing how to save so you can keep more of your money at retirement.

That's where we come in. We help people just like you cut your taxes so you can retire with confidence.

Step 1: Building a road map to meet your goals starts by determining where you are at today and understanding your vision of the future.

Step 2: We help you by creating a financial plan designed to secure your retirement by helping you cut your taxes and keep more of your money.

Step 3: No financial plan is effective unless it is successfully implemented. We will help you make your retirement dreams become reality!

Most people think it takes the stock market to build real wealth. Now you know your options. You can keep more money in your pocket by cutting your taxes and have peace of mind when you retire.

If you'd like us to help, just send an email to: **Jeffery.Palmer@prudential.com** and we will take it from there.

Jeffery J. Palmer

Jeffery Palmer offers financial planning and investment advisory services through Pruco Securities, LLC (Pruco), doing business as Prudential Financial Planning Services (PFPS). The Palmer Group was founded by Jeff Palmer who started in the financial service industry in 1990. Jeff began his quest in financial planning as a college student at Western Carolina University receiving his BSBA degree double majoring in Financial Planning and Computer Information Systems. After graduating from college with honors, he began his career with The Prudential Insurance Company of America.

Jeff for many years has been one of Prudential Financial Planning Services leading financial planners receiving many industry honors as well as multiple Vanguard Awards from The Prudential Insurance Company of America for excellence in financial planning. In 2004, 2008 and 2009, he was the number one financial planner in the nation for Prudential Financial Planning Services. This is no easy achievement for a small town boy residing in rural Western North Carolina especially when he is competing against colleagues around the country in many affluent cities.

Jeff's mission is to help people and create a life-long friendship with each client. He is there to celebrate their victories and will be there for them when the world seems to be crashing around them. Jeff spends many personal hours studying financial resources while learning and developing his skills as a financial planner to better assist clients in reaching their goals. He is client focused not Jeff focused. When it comes to helping secure his clients financial future, he endeavors not to leave anything to chance. Jeff is a Chartered Financial Consultant ChFC®. He holds the following securities registrations: Series 7, 6, 63 and 65. He holds the following insurance licenses: Life, Accident and Health, and Long-term care.

Jeff married his high school sweetheart, Kim and they have two children, Christina and Jack. Due to Christina being born with a birth defect called spina bifida, he has first-hand experience helping families with special needs planning. He serves on the Finance Committee and is a deacon at Biltmore Baptist Church where he has been a facilitator for Crown Financial ministries. He loves coaching his son's basketball and travel baseball teams through Upward Sports and Diamond Mine Baseball Training Facility. Jeff loves mountain biking, trout fishing, physical fitness, traveling and spending time with his family. Also, Jeff is an avid real estate investor but this is not part of his practice. Jeff is very proud of his heritage growing up in Andrews, North Carolina, a small town in the Appalachian mountains of Western North Carolina.

The Palmer Group is headquartered in Asheville, North Carolina. Jeff has a committed team who adheres to a professional code of ethics and regulatory compliance. Jeff and his team stay astute to the financial market place through active membership in many associations and strong industry alliances

Jeffery Palmer offers financial planning and investment advisory services through Pruco Securities, LLC (Pruco), doing business as Prudential Financial Planning Services (PFPS), pursuant to separate client agreement. Jeffery Palmer offers insurance and securities products and services as a registered representative of Pruco, and an agent of issuing insurance companies.

The Palmer Group is an independent organization and is not an affiliate of Prudential Financial. The Palmer Group sells life insurance products of Prudential Financials affiliated life insurance companies in addition to products of non-affiliated insurance companies.

0259205-00004-00

Jeffery Palmer offers investment advisory services as a representative of Prudential Financial Planning Services, a division of Pruco Securities, LLC (Pruco), and securities products and services as a Registered Representative of Pruco. 1-800-621-6690. The Palmer Group is not affiliated with Pruco. Other products and services may be offered by a non-Pruco entity. Neither The Palmer Group or Prudential or its affiliates are affiliated with any of the fore mentioned. Neither Prudential Financial, its affiliates, nor its financial professionals, render tax or legal advice. Please consult with attorney, accountant, and/or tax advisor for advice concerning your particular circumstances.

0278003-00002-00